EARTHCLOCK

EARTHCLOCK

a narrative calendar of nature's seasons

Anita Nygaard

with illustrations
by Paul Bauman

Stackpole Books

EARTHCLOCK

Copyright © 1976 by
Anita Nygaard

Published by
STACKPOLE BOOKS
Cameron and Kelker Streets
Harrisburg, Pa. 17105

Printed in the U.S.A.

Library of Congress Cataloging in Publication Data

Nygaard, Anita.
  Earthclock.

  1. Nature.   2. Outdoor recreation.   I. Title.
QH84.N9   500.9   75-31881
ISBN 0-8117-0547-1

Contents

When does the year begin? Properly speaking, there is no beginning, and therefore no end. Put a finger anywhere on the turning wheel, as the earth spins and turns on its axis, and there is, somewhere, some engagement of motion and activity. Nature does not stop moving, or stop tracing the endless patterns. Animals hibernate, but continue to breathe. Winter is a time of recession and retreat, but in those stony months the deer and resident birds struggle harder for a living, and cells attend the coming of light; almost biblically prophetic is the first warm clear day of February. Men arbitrarily decided to make January 1 a starting point (the god Janus ruled light and the day); naturalists point to the vernal equinox, but these are in part arbitrary decisions.

Spring is an event only in the temperate world; the tropics have only alternating cycles of rain and wind, and in the inhospitable polar world, summer comes abrupt on the retreat of winter. Only in a gentled zone of the captious earth is there the transition, the halting forward and back stages of growth and life that reach with tentative promise between dimness and brightness, death and hope.

Acknowledgments

The eternal sun . . . Mount Jefferson, a glowing mountain with a narrow summit like a royal observatory . . . a mountain lion whose eyes looked steadily across a forest clearing . . . the icy lake near Evolution wilderness, awakening and restorative, with a tangy grit in it . . . wild blueberries along a trail . . . coyote music at dusk . . . birds rising out of a tree like spray from a fountain . . . frost-smarting mornings by a campfire and a deer walking by following his breath . . . an ocean beach, intensity of sound and rocks and spray . . . the softness of quiet-dancing snowflakes . . .

The author acknowledges all the things in nature that never change (and are continually perversely changing) and are the solid shape and elusive patterns of reality.

Spring:
First Light

April 1

Patterns of April: the sphere—the egg and the seed, the first round swelling of blossom.

April 3

Nature is not benevolent, nature is just.

–John Burroughs, born April 3, 1837

April 4

After the long silence of winter, earth finds its voice. April is a medley of melodies.

11

Musicians have tried to set April to instruments—Stravinsky wrote the notes for the brazen discordant fervor of a pagan spring; Beethoven composed his mellow-flowing Pastoral; Delius heard the voice of the cuckoo. April is all of these, and has the pretty wistfulness of Puccini.

More than any other month, April is lyric, with the music of frogs, the twinkling steps of rainshowers in a jig dance. The white-throated sparrow whistles. Song emerges from the swollen throat of the spring peeper. Birds preen and display, all the time using their voices—most articulate of creatures, trilling, calling, chattering, their light soprano voices themselves pure ornaments of sound. Many tiny birds seem to possess voices bigger than themselves; they are all throat and vocal cords and humming wings. Everything speaks at once. Listeners have "heard" many human words in bird song; actually, these are patterns of sound, as geometrical as crystals or snowflakes, a symmetrical burst of cadence and fluting interruption, the unbreakable code. Insects hum. Smaller sounds: the scratch of birds on grass and brush.

The musical month. After keeping still for so long, creatures can no longer contain themselves and like the spilling stream, flood the air with sound.

If ears could hear, there would be the deeper sounds of the earth shifting and thawing and bending; perhaps at night the stars would crackle. In the morning there would surely be the thin high sounds—faint and far-away—of the moving clouds.

All the air is filled with the cheerful, impatient noise of nature.

April 5

In the thirties, a young boy on a farm in South Dakota, caught between barn and house, saw that he had underestimated the speed of an approaching tornado. It had appeared, it seemed, out of nowhere in the midst of all the rain and hail, and now was coming straight for him. All he could see was immense gray, the dark eyeless Thing itself. He did the only thing he could think of—Play dead! and threw himself flat on the ground. The tornado turned at the last minute and veered away, but a milk pail and a fork went flying from the boy's hands. ("Like the devil danced.")

April, a mild beneficent one in most of the country, is less gentle in the Midwest, striking at the earth with savage twisters. Tornadoes come into being when warm wet winds and cool dry currents collide; the plains east of the Rockies are their breeding ground. South Dakota, Oklahoma and Kansas are often hit; a savage tornado in Topeka killed and destroyed. The twister is the strongest wind on earth—300 to 600 miles per hour. It forms when the vortex drops out of a thundercloud and sucks into its path of vacuum air, dust, houses, cattle—anything in its way. To the boy who played dead in the tornado's path, and to people who have seen and heard it, the tornado is a twisting, riding tower, intense and frightening. The hard, high sound of the wind is as tense as the swaying blackness of the tower.

Weather observers now are able to predict some tornadoes, giving people enough warning to reach the safety of cellars and shelters, but still do not know exactly what causes a tornado or how it can be controlled. When the twister rides, people get out of the way.

April 6

Bluebirds appear, in pairs. This is the mating and nesting time for these birds, which are the bluest of birds, the clear bright blue that makes even blue jays look drab and makes these radiant birds the traditional symbol of happiness.

That bluebirds appear each spring, two by two, to nest and carry on the tradition of mate and family augurs well for the institution of marriage, as opposed to "meaningful relationships, and contracts." Man has, to an extent, copied his rites of courtship and his solemn nuptials, copied the amiable instinctual drives of the small creatures.

Bluebirds, however, are doubting Thomases in their homebuilding; vacillating and timorous, they will spend hours making up their minds on a nesting site choice, and have had property stolen out from under their noses by more daring birds.

April 7

Toads emerge from their winter burrows. A trembling call comes tentatively from the pool, still later another sound; then the inquiring voices are joined by the other calling toads. The males are the vocalists, trilling and questioning the air. Love! Love! They are hungry for mates, palpitating and tremulous with spring-dazed desire. By the end of April, all the males are in full voice, and a chorus of longing and rhapsody swells from the waters.

April 8

NO MIRACLES

April offers the surest proof of immortality. The month is one of new leaves on wind-stripped trees, new green on the frost-killed plants, the perennial rebirth of spring. Expected and familiar as it is, the cycle of reawakening always seems new and fresh; spring comes every year as a surprise. People speak of the miracle of spring. No miracle; nature keeps doing the same things in predictable fashion.

Things may run imperfectly, or disappointingly, or in fits and starts (the blind, groping mechanism of evolution), but never is there direct intervention from the implacable Other. There are no miracles in nature. Always the familiar, the repeated, for centuries, to go on, to endure. If one branch of the tree fails, another flourishes and grows; if this planet burns itself out, a new planet will be born in another corner of space.

The persistence of life is its most astonishing quality, its quality of inevitability, the fireweed that springs up in burned-over land; the most casual, accidental-appearing chances of life are proof of its durability.

Nature continues to operate on its own laws. Never on this earth the miracle. Men have long populated the earth and the skies with fairies and trolls and angels, but there is no supernatural. Nature is consistent, and sufficient to itself.

There is a correctness, a propriety to April, which is the fleshing out of nature and the visible reenactment of justice.

No need to go looking for signs and wonders; it is all there in the plowed field, the clouds that part after the rain. The most reverent eye is the one that searches the morning sky for the return of sun. April may be haphazard and apparently without design—a cloudy, windy day on the heels of one mellow with the taste of spring—but the cycle is inalterably repeating itself.

Ye must be born again is a universal command, as much a law as that which states that all things die.

April 9

Violets are the flower of spring, and when the poet celebrates spring, he sings of violets.

"That queen of secrecy, the violet," Keats wrote, for many violets bloom in the deep wood, a warming and refreshing sight as the snows creep away. But there are violets that love sunny banks, and violets crowding in the dooryard, and violets alight in wet meadows. With a look of delicacy and fragility, violets are the very pattern and color and scent of frail, fragrant spring, but surprisingly hardy and enormously varied; there are even white and yellow violets. All are prizes— the rewards of spring's light and gently warming days—garlands for amateur poets as well.

April 11

This is the cruelest month.

Nature has one purpose now, reproduction, accomplished in crude and violent couplings, in burgeoning leaf, in birds bursting and calling with the desire to mate and repeat themselves, in seeds dividing and multiplying.

The process—dizzy, total—repeats and spreads in perfect organization. In numbers, birds mate and insects multiply, the earth shines with dazzle of leaf and bud, there is a gloss to the sky.

An illusion, of course, for death has to follow life, and all this display of life seems ironic and hopeless to people who have lost hope.

Spring goes by faster for the old; every year the process speeds, until one year it seems the process has been accomplished overnight and the entire world is awash with living forms.

Nostalgia visits the old and the not-so-old for the youth that was like springtime, evanescent and fleeing from sight like something half-glimpsed out the corner of an eye, never totally realized. April is the time of half-forgotten hopes, dead and buried under the frozen winters, crushed in the hurry and race of spring to get nowhere.

April dazzles with its tender moods of sunlight and breeze; charms and seduces with blossom and birdcall. Often people look at this display of porcelain sky and enraptured birds, feeling themselves no part of it, consider it all an illusion and themselves disillusioned, and go home and explode bullets into their temples. April is also the month of suicide.

April 12

A sudden hailstorm dances and skips on an April afternoon, a shower of white pebbles bouncing off the warm ground, proof that winter is not yet totally gone.

The falling hail has an odd, impromptu sound like a nervous crowd clapping. No permanence to the hail, lying brilliantly in spilled profusion. The stones, cold and hard, melt quickly; they have a temporary, flashy beauty, swiftly vanished. There is no substance to a spring storm, which is all pretense and bluff.

April 13

The calving season for the American bison. (The more familiar term—buffalo—is actually a misnomer.) When the pioneers came West they forged their way through herds of these mighty animals, cutting them down like trees to clear the land. Millions of the great bison had flourished in dust-ridden clouds, the thunder of their hooves like the heartbeat of the plains itself. Marching in a herd, bison were a dark heaving sea of massed bodies; one herd was estimated to be 25 miles long and 50 miles deep, taking days to pass through a valley, the sound of their moving a rumble that shook the earth.

The animal was a way of life for the Plains Indians, who ate the fresh meat, ate the dried pemmican, made beds and blankets of the hides, made spoons from horns, and whips from the tails. The tribes prayed that these animals would live forever. Both Indian and buffalo were doomed as the white men came West. The brooding great spirit that darkened the plains with bison bodies vanished.

Carnage was casual and nearly complete. Buffalo were slaughtered from train windows. Carcasses were left to rot in the sun; sometimes the horns of the slain became tipsy and ignoble hatracks. In perhaps twenty years, the bison were reduced to a few wary, maddened strays; of the herd that had fled to Yellowstone to escape, 21 remained.

Now, a few live in protected reserves; a few buffalo are bred on ranches, and buffalo meat is available in restaurants that advertise themselves as preserving the traditions of the West.

No longer God of the plains, the American bison is now only a shaggy, large beast, grotesque with his thick-shouldered mane and his crescent horns. Small-eyed and fierce, he seems to live with the dimming memories of rage and power, attacking an occasional stalled car or a hiker in search of a snapshot. Black Diamond, an immense bull, lived in Central Park Zoo (a real buffalo, folks!) and was the model for the buffalo nickel—token memento of the past.

Some of the most interesting and vivid experiments of nature are gone forever, or exist only in saddened diminished remnants— the bison, the dinosaur, the condor. Even Smiley, the saber-toothed cat, left only a few moldering bones in the La Brea tar pits. In retrospect, at least, the Neanderthal, the Australopithecus, and the original American Indians seem to have possessed a vividness, a pungency, and an originality largely lost today, as if the efforts of evolution were to produce a bland and colorless mixture of race and species.

The great spirit to whom the Indians prayed has become a joke.

April 15

In warm wet weather, weeds spring up and out by the hundreds, moving to take advantage of every bit of space. One afternoon, seemingly, there is only the bare space of ground; the next day, tall weeds are everywhere. The hardiest, most adaptable, fastest-growing, most resistant of plants are those called weeds. These are the plucky heroes of the botanical world that in true Horatio Alger style, grow and flourish in ragged crowds or as solitary stubborn individuals. The gardener curses dandelion and chickweed and thistle; if he could he would post his land as ranchers do and hang the pelts of slaughtered plants along the fence. Weeds respond to his pulling and digging by growing more vigorously. For some weeds, it takes brutal doses of chemical killer to stop their lively rampage—poison that will also cripple the soil and destroy other plants and visiting birds. Still, weeds are a matter of definition; the slender horsetail reed grows exuberantly beyond its boundaries, an odd pencil-like plant, striped lustrous green, with no leaves or flowers, and finally a gardener pulls up the entire plant, having had enough.

April 16

A watery month as rain splashes from the sky and swells mounting lakes and streams, already filled with snow melt.

Life ripens in the fresh waters: insects appear in abundance and become banquets for fish, who struggled through a skimpy winter and now prosper on insect rations and become lively again.

Freshwater snails lay their eggs, fifty or more at a time, in a gelatinous mass, from which the perfectly formed shells will appear. The yellow perch spawns. The female newt lays one egg at a time, each tiny capsule securely fastened to a water plant. It will be a long season for the newt; she will in time lay several hundred eggs—at the rate of a half-dozen or so a day. Painted turtles come up from the muddy bottom and begin to swim about, from time to time emerging to rest on a surfaced log or rock. An exchange of fish now in April-freshened waters as native fish crowd toward the sea, and the migrants—shad and herring—make the journey from the sea to inland watercourses.

April 17

White snow, lying innocent and untracked on a mountain slope, can thunder down, roaring, and killing like a runaway express train. Any slope over twenty degrees can avalanche, as the weight of the snow pulls away from the mountainside.

Skiers and climbers have been killed as they crossed moderate slopes, or killed while they slept in their tents when early dawn avalanches fell.

April is the treacherous month; warming sun, following days of snowfall, peels the mountain as casually as an onion. Or, high winds shift and pack snow; a fracture line shudders across the slope, and a slab avalanche pulls the entire slope downhill. Climax, or terminal avalanches, are the end accomplishments of April, as entire snowpacks, aged and wet, pull away from the ground. Mount Saint Helens in Washington has an impressive toll; in April, 1975, five university climbers were heaped in a mass burial when they camped below an avalanche path.

Avoiding obvious avalanche terrain (the paths where snowslide is an annual event) is an elementary precaution, but few routes are 100 percent safe; the spring slopes beckon to skiers and early season climbers, and risk is a component of even the simplest adventure.

Other precautions are possible. Ski through timber rather than open snow, if possible. Climb a slope in single file, rather than traversing and exposing the slope to repeated friction and pressure. Ski from safety island to safety island (trees, outcroppings of rocks). Cross slopes high towards the top.

Travel lightly, ready to ditch equipment, carrying ski poles without wrist straps, and wearing unfastened pack straps.

Pessimistic (or prepared) skiers trail avalanche cords—thin ropes fifty to seventy-five feet long, in bright colors, the end attached to the skier marked. If he is caught in an avalanche, the cord will tend to rise to the surface, thus being to rescuers a flag of the buried skier's location.

A skier who intends to live long probes—and listens. Suspicious warnings: the hollow sound of unsettled snow, faint fracture lines breaking ahead of the ski tips. Anticipate trouble; the best ski tourers are bad weather travelers, relying on colder temperatures for safety.

Avalanches are fast; in seconds an entire slope may be stripped of the top layer of snow. Caught in a white racing sea, no skier can outrun the avalanche, but tries to get to the side and let the fury past.

The sound of the avalanche—a heavy and gusty shudder as the mountain breaks away—will never be forgotten by anyone who has heard it. In any catastrophe, panic kills. Skiers and climbers have escaped death by staying calm, using swimming motions to stay on the surface, shielding the face with hands and arms to form air pockets, and saving energy, if buried, by waiting for rescue calmly. It is possible to survive for hours even if submerged—a thought to hold onto while waiting for rescue in a white soundless grave.

April 18

The weeping willow hangs its delicate drooping branches along the stream. In early spring, the green-yellow catkins are inconspicuous, easily mistaken for foliage. Slender-leaved, long-branched, the tree has a deceptively frail and ornamental look, a tree for serene oriental gardens and wistful moods.

An illusion only; the tree is a stout, fast-growing, easily propagated opportunist. In yards, the roots spread at a furious rate, crowding and choking out other plants, and cracking concrete driveways. Willow chairs left outside in the yard have been known to take root.

April 19

GOD'S WRATH

The earth snaps under shifting pressures. Rock bursts and heaves with a twanging reverberation. It can be silent, gentle, barely felt (a chandelier swings into motion), or the earthfloor pulled out, under a sound like an approaching train, and an entire city destroyed in less than a minute, as houses come crashing down into rubble.

Earthquakes were once thought to be expressions of God's displeasure with people, but churches have toppled and the church bells set to ringing in crazed echoes.

First comes the primary wave, a great retching spasm. An S-wave follows, twisting, and traveling half as fast. Aftershocks may linger for hours or weeks.

Numerous theories have been suggested as to the causes of earthquakes, which are ultimately symptoms of the earth's distress. The quake may be the release of shifts and strains, or the moving of tides in the solid world.

Some of the most devastating earthquakes have appeared in early spring: Anchorage, Alaska, March 27, 1964; San Francisco, April, 1906; California, April 19, 1892; an April quake in the sixties astonished residents of normally tranquil Seattle.

Hollister, California is the earthquake capital of the world, a dubious distinction, but one which the residents feel possibly gives them insurance against a major disaster, with the repeated small shocks that take up much of the earth's strain.

California has always been an unstable land. Eighteen twelve was the "year of the tremblers"; an immense mission was crushed, and the earthquake hurled stones and tiles into the air.

The San Andreas fault lies like a sleeping snake, coiled along the length of California. A few people wonder idly when it will strike again.

April 20

The dandelion is making a comeback (a surprise to those who thought it had never gone away, and with aggrieved expressions, wrench it out of the lawn each spring).

Actually the flower is attaining status as a perfectly respectable vegetable/wine/grain/home remedy. Occasionally, mail-order nurseries with more inventiveness than ethics have advertised, "Buy the Golden Crown! In a few weeks see your yard become a showplace of sturdy gold bloom! Hardy, fast-growing—" The lion's tooth, most ill-regarded of flowers, prospers by doing away with such discriminating niceties as sexual reproduction, as Krutch has described so chillingly, with all its alarming implications of a plant world reverting to standardized and heartless mass production.

Make the most of a spring crop of dandelions:

Make coffee (minus the caffeine). Carefully collect the deep tenacious taproots, scrub the roots clean, and roast at 300° until brittle and a deep brown at the interior. Grind in a coffee mill or blender and brew.

Make salad. Use the young leaves and stems that appear just above the root at ground level. Slice the white rosette off close to the crown. Wash, soak in cold water, and drain. Serve with a tangy dressing.

Make a vegetable dish. Harvest the high green leaves just before the plant blooms, steam a scant five minutes, and serve with salt, pepper and butter. (Better than spinach.)

Make tea. (The gypsies say it's kind to the liver and soothes rheumatism.) Use the large, mature leaves, dark and strong-bodied, and dry thoroughly in a paper bag. Crumble the dried leaves, using a heaping teaspoon to brew each cup of tea.

Make wine.

Dandelion Wine I

Pour one quart boiling water over one quart of clean, fresh dandelion flowers. Allow to stand three days. Strain and add peel and juice of two oranges, one lemon, and a half-pound of diced raisins (optional). Boil twenty minutes. Cool to lukewarm, stir in one pound sugar and half a yeast cake (Chablis yeast produces a smooth, dry wine). Allow to stand three days in a warm place, strain, and let rest, covered, two or three weeks until fermentation stops. Decant and bottle. A year's wait improves the wine.

Dandelion Wine II

Pour four pints of water over three pints dandelion flowers. Let stand six days; then strain through muslin. Boil the liquor a half-hour, with two pounds sugar, one lemon, one sweet orange, and one bitter orange. Let stand in casks or half-gallon bottles for six months; then rebottle.

People who really like dandelions and their uses are growing dandelions as cultivated plants—ordering highly developed seeds from such growers as Burpee. The dandelion that drives some persons to choking fits of frustration now grows in tidy domestic rows; soon there will be prizes given for the prettiest dandelion of the year.

April 21

A VISION OF LIGHT

John Muir was born April 21, 1838, in Dunbar, Scotland, and for many people has never died.

Certainly his words live on, for mountaineers and hikers, choice actual morsels, carried as refreshment in the mouth: "Climb the mountains and get their good tidings." "Yonder stands South Dome . . . clothed in light and filled with intelligence like a God." Of Yosemite's waterfalls in the spring: "The snow is melting into music."

Muir came to America as a child and grew up on a Wisconsin farm, intensely inventive, curious, interested in things mechanical. But an accident injured one eye, and Muir made a resolve: he would devote his life to the "study of the inventions of God."

He went to California in 1868 and began an odd lifetime career of ill-assorted jobs and his one real task, the observation and recording of nature, in prose that sounded like poetry and spread the word of nature to both scientists and laymen.

All his life Muir carried the baggage of a gloomy Protestant upbringing which saw nature as savage and undisciplined and faintly sinister, but Muir set about cannily to reform the world, telling it instead of the free glories of wild nature.

Later, he virtually rejected his ancestors' religion: "No dogmas taught by the present civilization seem to form so insuperable an obstacle in the way of a right understanding of the relations which culture sustains to wilderness as that which regards the world as made especially for the uses of man."

He was a sheepherder who became angry when he saw the destruction his charges did and called them "hoofed locusts." He did subsistence work at a sawmill—anything to be near his beloved Yosemite, and later tramped Yosemite for six years, carrying little more than the bedroll and beans which have become traditionally attached to this legendary figure. For him, Yosemite was a vision of light, in the incomparable sheen of that granite range.

He was a travel-light tramp, and a poet, but he was a better scientist than the dour Professor Whitney, and Muir was the first to assess the true glacial origin of Yosemite's rocks.

Eye to eye with nature, Muir adventured and discovered: a bear, or a storm, or a squirrel, a water ouzel, or a glacier.

His journeys were bold; he scrambled nervily on airy rock, crept carefully down slippery rock beside a waterfall, climbed the obdurate steepness of Half Dome in winter.

People were more disappointing: a meeting with the admired Emerson was unsatisfying and troubling; marriage only partly domesticated the great adventurous spirit of Muir.

Muir, who pressed a program of vigorous forest preservation, and stands in the history of conservation as its archangel, was an avatar—the message that visits the earth like a meteor. He fought the battle between "landscape righteousness and the devil." He founded the Sierra Club, which works in militant fashion on conservation issues. He was not always successful; he lost the fight to stop Hetch-Hetchy from being converted into a reservoir.

His work is unfinished.

"I will brood above the Merced Mountains like a cloud, until all the rivers of this mighty system are fully restored, each in its channel, harmonious as a song."

April 22

This month, in a secluded den, the red fox is born. From this peaceful nursery he and his brothers and sisters will emerge to a precarious, short life.

He has been called wily or cunning; many writers have credited him with enjoying the chase as much as the men and dogs who chase him. Aesop immortalized him with a sly and sharp sagacity, and modern fables tell of his propensity for eating chickens and in general leading a merry chase. Men seem to reserve their strongest hatreds and hostilities for doglike creatures whom they cannot tame; only the domestic dog is allowed to share the woods and fields. For Reynard: bullets, and the entire redcoated panoply of the hunt, a traditionally royal pastime which commoners enjoy.

One hunt ended in disaster—not for the fox, which appeared to be laughing as he went his way, but for a horse; at the last minute the fox swerved aside from a cliff, the frightened horse buckled and plunged, crashing into rocks and throwing the rider. The hunt ended with a dead horse and a bruised and angered man, and several perplexed hounds.

A hiker rounded a corner on a forest trail and came upon a red fox quietly seated in the tree shadows, surveying the domain of woods and sky. The fox's face for a minute registered perfect astonishment as he scrambled up, and then what appeared to be a teasing look of challenge and curiosity, before it gracefully moved away, looking back twice.

One of the most beautiful of creatures, the fox is one of the saddest and limpest dead, as corpse or stiffened fur, without the flash of movement and agility that filled the red-burnished coat and the bouncing plume of tail. Despite the fables, he lives mostly on mice and berries and insects, and his wits do not save him from occasional attacks of wolf or eagle, or the greater killer, rabies. The male is a courageous and protective parent, sleeping in the open to guard his young, and changing his voice from a bark to a fierce scream when threatened.

The pretty, pointed face is one of the pleasantest surprises to see in a chance encounter, for the fox is one of the few animals who will directly return a man's look. In an eye-to-eye encounter, the fox wins. The bright quick stare he gives man is not inquisitive only but provocative, a feisty and forward tilt of sharp eye and nose, a look that seems to say, "Dare me if you can."

April 23

All about is the rich green determination of April. There is a muscular, purposeful activity to April, the swelling, straining drive and push of leafing, growing things. Sunlight and showers like pulleys act on the earth, to incite the leap of blossom and bud. After a rainshower the sun comes out again and visibly the earth brings forth its young.

All about is the rich, sweet smell of spring, as pervasive and animal and alive a smell as the heady scent of success.

April 24

WILD LOVE

April is the natal month for some residents—mice, wildcats, raccoons. Other animals are mating. Nature is a grossly sexual adventure, practical and vigorous, boisterously and blindly concerned with the business of reproduction.

The great purpose and accomplishment of sex is not so much reproduction itself—many species of animals and plants have no differentiated sexes and nevertheless reproduce themselves—but variety. The intermix of traits produces different plants, new animals, new humans. Sex is the ultimate risk; each mating and subsequent birth is a gamble on genes meeting genes.

Love is a willingness to take that gamble, and a moment's yielding (at least)—in its simplest definition, a trust or confidence. The trust may be misplaced (the female spider eats her mate). Yet the sensory itch may be colored by affection, or what appears to be affection, and is at least trust and reliance.

Wolves mate and become monogamous families—the most loyal of husbands and fathers. Damselflies clasp each other in the air. Mating birds provide a family portrait of mutual support. Domestic dogs, to all practical purposes, fall in love with the neighborhood bitch and moon after the scent of her passing. An old Tom, cauliflower-eared and pugnacious, may be accompanied everywhere by a dutiful mate. Elk bat at each other with furious horns to win the privilege of selecting their mates. Even fish, normally considered unresponsive ("cold fish") have their moments: the male stickleback glows red and iridescent blue-green in ceremonial courtship. Fish of the cichlid group live a devoted family life with both caring for the young (a routine humans are slow to adopt).

Like meeting unlike is the sum and gist of love, whether it lasts a few seconds or for years. Time duration is no measure of the lightning's power. The eruption of love is the exchange, and that is the same for all forms of life.

Freud is in some disfavor now, and few psychiatrists would trace all human behavior to the sexual drive, but it is impossible to claim that affection, or loyalty, or even companionship can spring to being in a vacuum, divorced from the moody impulses of the body. Without that genital storm, no stimuli exists to prod into being what is romantically idealized as the nobler passions.

The brain with its sensations of love is end-product of the crudest coupling; the mind is nurtured in the crotch. Ultimately, all evolution rests on the beginnings, and the first step is the coming together of the male and female. All life is that search for the *other*; every bird (singing gently, lyrically); every dog, scratching insanely at the door to be let out; every bull gone ornery and mean with throbbing penis; every wolf, devotedly guarding the den; every human impaled on his loneliness, is asking, Where are you?

April 25

ARBOR DAY

Plant a tree for the sake of the world. The world is overfilled with motionless things, concrete, buildings, storefronts, power poles, signs, billboards. A tree moves with the wind, and grows toward the light. (Natives in parts of the world believe that it is the tree itself which pushes the air from it.) A tree is soft silence in a too-noisy city, and a warm, living thing to touch. Let there be a population explosion of trees to refresh and renew the world.

April 27

April is not all flowers and showers and pretty green buds.

Insects are resuming their interrupted lives: bumblebee queens, survivors of last year, are greedily foraging for nectar, storing up energy for the domestic duties ahead.

Ladybird beetles emerge from their bowers. From under old boards, woolly bears sleepily uncurl.

The females of the spring cankerworm climb up the trees to take their stations here; the males, equipped with wings, will search them out. The eggs of the tent caterpillar hatch, and little silken nests appear on wild cherry branches. Ants and flies begin the work of rebuilding and food gathering, and soon will flourish in companionable crowded clouds. Tree borers start work again. Moths and butterflies are about—paler, less distinct forerunners of summer's gaudy display.

All is industry now in the insect world, after the months of inactivity. Back to work! Does the butterfly admire the flower? That, supposedly, is a privilege reserved for man, with his capacity for leisure. For insects, it is a workaday world.

April 28

April is a time for following the rainbow.

The rainbow a person sees is his own. Each rainbow is, in a

sense, a personal vision—or an illusion, depending upon the point of view.

April is a sometime thing—an elusive, captious, unsettled, can't make up its mind vacillation between rain and sun. ("April showers bring May flowers.") The ground, wetted and drenched intermittently, receives the benison of surprisingly strong, warm sun.

It is just this now you see it, now you don't combination of raindrops and sunrays that produce that mysterious bending bridge called the rainbow. A rainbow can appear on the far horizon, or be as close as the lawn sprinkler. Essentially, it is reflected light, as sunrays hit drops of water.

As sunrays strike the outer edge of the round raindrops, the rays are refracted and dispersed into different lengths of light waves, thus producing the various colors. Each color is formed by rays reaching the observer's eye at certain angles. At an approximate 42° angle, the eye sees red. Other color bands below the red occur at various lower angles and present shades of orange, yellow, green, blue, and violet.

The number of colors, and the width of their bands in the bow, depend on the size of the raindrops—and the observer. As the rainbow is visible only when a person forms a certain angle with the raindrops, it may reflect red-green to one person, and at the same time, yellow-blue to another individual standing some feet away at a different angle.

Once it was believed that a pot of gold stood at the foot of a rainbow. Hard to find; when a person moves, the rainbow moves too. No one can look up and see a rainbow over his head, for as he walks a new rainbow is formed as light strikes the raindrops differently. The retreating rainbow is actually a new one formed each time by the different position. Chasing rainbows is frustrating work.

A double rainbow happens when sunlight at about a 51° angle from the eye enters the bottom of the waterdrops and undergoes double internal reflection—bouncing twice inside the raindrop. The second reflection or bounce produces a second perfect bow—with colors precisely in the opposite order of those in the first bow.

Light itself seems both form and activity, being particlelike and wavelike at the same time. The particles, or photons, are capable of animated behavior—minute pieces of matter acting much like waves— lively stage hands producing great effects.

Early men considered the stunning and transient rainbow a hostile omen of bad luck. Others believed it was a great snake that swallowed water and held back the rain.

Through the years the rainbow—a bridge that bends back on

itself and leads again to the earth—has become a charming and feckless promise: it will rain no more. The promise of sun, glittering, illusory and personal vision as it is, is in each bright band of the bow.

April 29

Spring floods are not totally accidents of nature. The karma of human destiny also invites unexpected consequences in the natural world.

Flooding occurs in the valleys as the snows melt at higher elevations, swelling the rivers, and spring rains add to the weight of the descending waters.

If the slopes are timbered, trees serve as a check on the waters rushing to the valley. On a heavily forested slope, trees divert and delay the flow, not ordinarily suffering much themselves, unless too great a weight of water, coming too swiftly, erodes the soil and weakens root systems.

However, where man has cut the trees and opened the hillsides, leaving them bare and exposed to all the events of the seasons, the melting snows and the rains find nothing to arrest their headlong journey.

Then the farmers and residents consult the swollen gray belly of the river and look worriedly at the foundations of their houses, and newscasters report the rising river level.

If conditions are right, for nature—not for man—a flood fills the plain and valley as the river bursts out of its cage.

Disaster has destroyed many a misplaced optimism. Floods (unlike the lightning of proverbs) do strike repeatedly at the same spot, and dwellers in low-settling valleys find themselves unwilling hosts to the same powerful yearly visitor. New hastily built houses perched unsteadily on shifting land-fill are picked up and tossed around like kindling.

Then the flood is an animal, amorphous and mesozoic, like some primal monster of the sea. Turgid and without compassion, the dim brute of water moves blindly across and over everything in its path, taking and destroying. The spring flood in Vanport, Oregon took human lives, as well as flimsy wartime houses that bent and buckled under the seizing waters.

Still, floods can be beneficial. The flood that follows a hurricane opens and invigorates the forest. Fallen trees and limbs shelter the woods animals, are the natural food of the forest floor, and in the open spaces they left, give newly sun-drenched room for young growth to thrive.

Floods that burst the man-made seams of the valley redistribute the soil, and where the ground was thin and tired, fill the land with new vigor. On these dense black deltas will grow the richest of crops, the brightest of flowers. From one point of view, nature rearranges things to best advantage.

April 30

THINGS TO DO ON AN APRIL DAY

1. Walk in a rain shower—and feel the cool surprise of bland, lightly touching drops, a rain that brings no harm.

2. Plant flower seeds.

3. Hike up a foothill and get the first taste of exertion and spring air that is literally balmy, a soothing refreshment to winter-weary lungs.

4. Stare at birds. Knowledgeable hobbyists adept at identifying and counting and labeling, articulate in Latin names, go birding. Amateurs and sentimentalists are bird-watchers, simply observing birds for the fun of it. Be a bird-watcher.

5. Take a favorite dog for a walk. After a spell of housebound inactivity any reasonably ambitious dog goes spring-crazy on all those tantalizing new smells arising from the warming loosened earth.

6. Sit back and do nothing. Let the brain go into low gear, idle and unoccupied. Become a vegetable; like a plant sense the rightness of just being and growing.

◇◇◇

May 1

May Day was for years a sentimental American custom; now such rituals as the maypole dance and the hanging of May baskets on doors seem quaint and old-fashioned.

Girls' colleges traditionally have chosen a May queen; she is crowned after the girls dance around the maypole, weaving in and out of the brightly colored ribbons.

The May queen, an older girl, enjoys the brief pleasures of royalty—"Of all the glad New year, mother, the maddest merriest day."

She is of course reenacting the role of Flora, the goddess of flowers. The festival was instituted in early Rome, about 238 B.C., and was celebrated from April 28 to May 3. The maypole was no doubt a symbol associated with fertility. Druids celebrated the feast of Bel on May 1 (Bel is identified both with the Old Testament Baal and with Apollo). The festival of Floralia flourished in Europe and in England, and the sprightly merrymaking was imported to America.

Puritans frowned on such activities; a Governor Endicott of Massachusetts in 1660 led men to chop down a maypole.

In later years, celebrations of May and the fullblown approach of blossoming summer became more sweetly genteel: solemn young girls interweaving among the ribbons, children taking their delicate flower baskets (perhaps an Easter egg or a candy or two along with the blooms)—pretty and innocent rites of spring, as guileless as the season.

May brings flocks of pretty lambs
Skipping by their fleecy dams.

–Sarah Coleridge

May 3

Now, in May, the earth is solvent. The soil feels different, young and generous; it crumbles easily to the hand. May is the month of fertility. A richness to the flowering green trees, and to the soil itself. Experienced gardeners kneel as if in obeisance, humbled, sense a communication from the warm and yielding earth which they now call friable. Most people, even city dwellers, feel a sense of surprise and restoration in touching and handling May-warmed earth; this is the original vault where the riches are stored.

May 5

Sign of life: the river fish are laying their eggs. Fecundity extends to the riverbank and to the deeps of the river. Fish too are impregnated with the desire to live and reproduce. The quietest brook is the scene of a population explosion. An appetite for fishing was installed early in man; place a boy beside a brook and almost instinctively he knows what to do. Rivers are at their best early in the morning, when mists are rising in the trees like silver breath. The river is by turns quiet, noisy, alarmingly cold, glinting warm in the sunlight, a perfect challenge.

May 6

Insects now are at full tilt reproducing themselves. The May beetle emerges now, having spent two or three years of its youth underground. It may emerge in June—when it is called, of course, the June bug. Relative of the scarab beetle—mysterious and intriguing to the Egyptians, who regarded its appearance from the earth as inexplicable as spontaneous generation—the beetle retains a fondness of memory of its underground youth as a white larva, or grub, now eating grass roots and wreaking destruction in newly plowed field land. Adults become bolder and eat the foliage of elms and oaks.

As if to make up for the years of darkness, the beetles, roaming at night, are attracted in swarms to electric lights.

May 7

Where do flowers get their names? From birds, wolves (the blue lupine was quite unfairly named after a wolf in the belief it was a harmful flower, ravishing the soil), from colors, frogs (ranunculus, or wild buttercup, was so christened by Pliny the Elder because it shares its habitat with frogs). The adder's tongue nods its yellow blossom, poised on a long stalk, in serpentine grace.

All the common elements of nature share the essential link—their common likenesses—and thus their names. Buttercup is also a member of the crowfoot family; the wild geranium is a cranesbill because of its long, beaklike seedpod. The columbine shares the name of the dove because the five deep red spurs which are nectar pouches had to early countryfolk the look of perching doves. The partridgeberry is of course devoured by the partridge.

May 8

No well-traveled roads lead between man and animals, but the distance is short. A dog starts in his sleep, yelps mightily in pursuit of a dream-cat. Evolution is not so much a ladder as an entire playground—witness the grand experiments that have failed; dinosaurs rotting in the tarpits under the metropolis. A number of communal spirits romp or grieve on the earth, in different guises of fur or flesh or feathers. Cells are cells, shared in unequal or differing distribution, but still of the same basic stuff. The religious who claim special creation should feel abashed at their own pretensions; God is guilty not so much of favoritism as of absent-mindedness or whimsy. It is a kind of narrowest patriotism to claim special privileges for humanity, but the evidence doesn't stand up; to be born inside a random human womb and inhabit for a little while the erect rib cage is possibly no better and not much different from playing the game inside eagle wings or even a dolphin's slippery chest.

At heart people know this to be true, and for that reason, both hunt and persecute animals and pamper their pets. The sudden shocks of recognition come in stealthy ways. The dreaming dog shares the same desires as man; one has only to look at an ape to sense our common heritage. Life is a grab bag of random chances and take-what-you-get bonuses or penalties; it is not necessarily a privilege to have been born a human. Animals perhaps sense this, too, and sometimes seem to look at men with amazement, even in tolerating the caress or fleeing the gun. Beyond language there is a community in sharing sounds and touch and the impartial earth.

> Animals are not brethren, they are not underlings; they are other nations, caught with ourselves in the net of life and time.
>
> –*Henry Beston*

May 10

The day is warm, fragrant with the pungent scent of fertility; pink blossoms have seemingly appeared overnight on the cherry trees, and the ground is loose and warm after gentle showers. On such a day the earth gives up its memories and treasures.

Still, conservation of nature applies equally to human relics.

Most people, if moderately decent and of reasonable good will, can understand and even practice the principles of conservation—if no conflict of self-interest is involved, as in strip mining and the development of a remote lake.

Yet the person conscientious in town not to litter, or the hiker careful with matches and campfire, discreetly refraining from the obscenity of a bough bed in a fragile alpine meadow, thoughtful not to kill wantonly any animal, may yield to the temptation to steal or deface the relics and records of our early inhabitants.

What is human seems, after all, ephemeral; man-made objects—even the highest of high-rise buildings or the burgeoning concrete arcs of freeways—have a temporary look. Man accustoms easily, in one sense, to the continual displacement and reconstruction of his man-made environment.

Certainly the early productions of man have the look of inconsequentiality, already vanishing, either disappearing to natural processes (the charred midden crumbles) or being stored in museums and archives where, despite the most meticulous of efforts and sophisticated acid-proof cases and temperature-controlled rooms, the baskets will eventually disintegrate, the manuscripts decay. There seems no permanent habitat for man or his efforts; entire libraries vanish in floods or fires, and time capsules, for all their solid air of witnessing to the future man's erratic and often graceless phenomena, may be obliterated by some natural event.

Temptation it is to take the arrowhead exposed by the newly eroded streambank after spring rain, or the metate found in a casual stroll. Rock paintings of the American Indians in the most shadowy and inaccessible of caves are a thrill to discover—and shortly bear the casual scribblings of the modern-day visitor alongside the provocative graffiti of some long-ago moccasined traveler.

Surface finds, of course, and most people would hesitate to tamper with a buried human skull—curio that it might be to display to friends. Still, the plains at one time were rich with arrowheads; of such tribes as the Chumash Indians little remains: great bowls, a few perfectly formed effigies, ochre drawings on rock as mysterious as nature's water writings on stone.

Yet these fragments left by time are a boon to the archaeologist who would seek to reconstruct. If he can discover what man was, where he lived and what he made, it may also be possible to foretell where man is going.

Nature replenishes and repeats in great leisurely cycles; predictions of the weather and the tides are written in past events. Evolving man, for all his technology, falls further and further behind his cultural development; the human brain is essentially the same as when it registered its first startled impressions from the darkened cave. The Neanderthals too buried their dead with flowers.

Taking a hand in evolution, the scientists may produce a future man totally behavior-modified, programed in his cells to a life of technology, made fit to survive by the intrusion of alien chemicals.

Such a man may in his future role look back on arrowheads and ollas as inventions of nature itself, perfected by the hands of an almost-human who was a simple and spontaneous creation of nature. The artifacts of man too are the flowering and fruition of an organic world.

Young people often sense this, and dress in Indian beads and skirts to mimic a sense of companionship with the earth, or a link to the fundamental satisfactions of nature. Few realize fully that they themselves are natural products; skin and glands and bones are the outpourings of a restless, seeking force, and the olla or projectile point is itself a product of creation as surely as a leaf, not to be picked up and tossed in a cigar box, or ploughed under.

Human relics must also be guarded and preserved, if anything is worth saving; an arrowhead is a record of evolution as much as a tree.

May 11

Now is the time for blossoms.

The trees are candy-colored, branches filled with blossoms like stars: apple, pear, cherry, dogwood, peach. Frail and delicately colored, the blossoms are easy victims to wind or rain; then they lie spilled on the lawn like the confetti of last night's merrymaking.

Bursting with light, they decorate block after block; great masses of blossoms make trees festive and soften the firm lines of branch and trunk, offering evanescent and shimmering bouquets to any passerby. Milk-white, pink and white, golden-glinting, the blossoms give the land a bridal look; the radiant nuptials of pollen and light. In smaller towns, it is still an amiable custom to drive the blossom route—admiring the short-lived burst of beauty.

May, despite its look of youth and delicacy, soft blush of maiden color and pastel dress like winsome bridesmaids, is not virginal; the mating has begun.

May 12

As nature celebrates, the time is appropriate for drinking May wine. Always a popular drink in Europe, the light refreshing wine is becoming known in America. The flavor derives from woodruff, a perennial herb known for its sweet fragrance. In Germany it is Waldmeister—the master of the woods.

Tiny—a precise delicate mat under the shade of trees—woodruff has oval leaves growing in whorls of eight. Later, in June and July, there will be the graceful white flowers, four-petaled and starlike.

In the spring, sprigs of fresh woodruff are gathered for the characteristic wine punch:

½ oz dried woodruff	*1 pt fresh strawberries*
(obtainable in many stores)	*1 bottle champagne*
4 bottles dry white wine	*2 cups sugar*
1 lg jigger benedictine	*1 pt sparkling water*
2 lg jiggers cognac	

Any good dry white wine serves, such as riesling, rhine, or dry sauterne.

Place dried woodruff in a wide-mouthed jar, open 1 bottle dry white wine, and pour over. Seal tightly. Steep eight hours.

Pour all well-chilled liqueurs and wines, including woodruff steeped in wine, into a punch bowl. Dissolve sugar in sparkling water, and add. Finally, add strawberries, and sprigs of fresh woodruff.

Celebrate spring.

May 14

The white hills of Lompoc in southern California were legendary before the Spanish conquistadores of the 1700s and the Franciscan padres who built the mission of La Purisima in 1787. In a rolling pastoral setting, hills like arrested waves slowly rising from the ocean, kindling brown in summer and emerald green in the spring, the chalky cliffs are odd, abrupt interruptions, gleaming on translucent May days like incongruous snow glaciers.

Not till a century after European settlement did people recognize that the magical white hills held a deposit of potentially useful diatomaceous earth.

The diatom—an aquatic single-celled alga or flowerless plant—grew in the billions in the Miocene period, as long as twenty million years ago, when much of the California coast lay below sea level. In that quiet archipelago of low islands and lagoons, the diatom, hardly visible in itself, a tiny floating plant living in a hard glass case of opaline silica, flourished and died, and quietly laid its skeleton to rest in the earth as the sea yielded to the land. Organic matter decomposed and fed other organisms; nature's most common cycle was repeated. Under a microscope, the diatom skeleton is highly ornamented and symmetrically patterned, a complex and many-roomed jewel. Such an intricate geometry of design astonishes and appalls—why this elaborate virtuoso arrangement of cells on the smallest scale? The beauty is an affront to eyes that need a microscope to see it. Nature takes infinite trouble with small things.

Centuries of rain washed pure the alternating masses of troughlike strata and arched strata, exposing white outcroppings that were the flags marking deposits hundreds of feet deep. Now, the strange white earth gives up its ancient secrets to all those prosaic purposes available to man's ingenuity.

Diatomaceous earth becomes: filters in the processing of sugar syrups, beer, drinking water, pharmaceuticals; filters in swimming pools, an abrasive in toothpaste, and an ingredient in lacquers, paints, polishes, plastics. A common use: insulation. Industry thrives on the diatom.

Still, any use of diatomaceous earth is based ultimately on the fossil itself. The tiny skeleton, for all its size—a scarce few microns in diameter—is incredibly rigid and strong. Loose fossils, massed in powder, do not pack together until man applies great force. The very low apparent density of the powder—only about ten pounds per cubic foot—is just this interlocking, interweaving of pores and voids, the tiny rigid cells of old fossils locked forever in their incredible stationary dance. (And nature, in a clownish mood, has put some of these diatoms in odd, tantalizing forms: owls, surrealistic dragonflies, fishlike shapes.) A random improvisation of structure? Each diatom is individual, like a snowflake; each diatom reproduces itself with perfect exactness.

May 16

"When lilacs last in the dooryard bloomed," Whitman wrote of these flowers that have a stately look, great proud heads of bloom, and yet an undeniable soft familiarity of appeal.

Now in May lilacs come into their full prime across the country. Most right-living neighborhoods can claim two or three of these beauties at least; lilac bushes grow easily and have a charming easy habit of adaptability to their surroundings, looking at ease beside a frowzy cottage or a grand old mansion.

Lilacs are at the same time the most regal and democratic of flowers. The color of royalty, with the added fillip of a soft persuasive fragrance—a ladylike sachet scent; many Americans still remember a childhood in which lilac bushes figured as flags of spring. Less assertive than the rose, lilacs are undemanding and easy to live with.

After a rain, lilacs appear to share the disappointment or the passing rebuke; the bushes droop. Sun comes out again and the lilacs raise their heads once more, gently yet proudly, as befits a flower everyone knows and trusts without thinking to be there, firm sign of hope. Long live the lilac.

May 18

Patterns for May: The blossom, fragile and profuse, bursting in froth and fluff or in perfect miniature starflower shapes. Fossils like incredibly small blossom shapes imprisoned in white chalky earth.

May 19

He has been called the "king of song," by naturalist Edward Forbush; he is a competent and diligent singer, spending most of his time these May days in bursts and patterns and displays of song, but for all that, he does not appear to take his singing very seriously. At his best (or worst) he is an industrious copycat, imitating robins or meadowlarks or any other bird that happens along; he has even imitated phonographs, pianos, roosters, and the mailman's whistle.

The mockingbird is found throughout most of the country, star performer from California to Kansas to the pine woods of Arkansas. His scientific name is *Mimus polyglottos*—bird of many tongues. The flash of the gray, white-winged body— usually 10½ inches long with its great tail—as he leaps from lookout perch to another branch, is barely more than a second's interruption in the continuing recital. On a soft May night, before dawn lifts the sky, windows bang shut; a mockingbird has sung too diligently at his post.

Nesting not far from the ground, perhaps no more than ten feet high in thicket or hedge, the singer pays the other birds the flattery of imitation but is as bold and clever in defending his territory: he sings *Ha, ha. Ha, ha*. The clear light voice guards the eggs—four to six, pale bluish-green and speckled with red-brown spots.

The voice is showy and imitative, an aggressive display of trills and high notes, making up in prolific production for any lack of inventiveness. Little of a poet on his own, though he does have his original cadenzas and extravaganzas, the mockingbird borrows all the sounds around him to put on his pretty show.

Still, there is a pensive quality to the light, high, tireless voice. Years ago a woman would sing (and the sound was plaintive in its remembering):

I'm dreaming now of Hally, sweet Hally . . .
Listen to the mockingbird, Listen to the mockingbird
Still singing where the weeping willows wave.

May 21

The earthworm is the underground railway of good gardens, transporting nutrients and rendering the soil fertile and lively. He is a sign of good earth; lacking him, foresighted gardeners buy a family of earthworms.

The worm's role in the process of converting and building: he eats minute particles of soil and returns the digested matter or castings to the hole of the burrow, and in his tunnelings and sorties cultivates and tills the soil with his efficient, sensitive, bristle-hooked body.

A faithful and industrious gardener, the earthworm—a slender pink-brown no more than a finger's length—is capable of great subterranean activities.

May 22

Composting is basic to serious gardening (or even the most casual). It can go on all year; it is essentially rewarding—there is a tidy sense of propriety and frugality to the process, in returning material to the earth and watching the cycle of decomposition and change. Last year's garden builds the stuff of next year's bloom and show.

There have been many recipes and directions written for composting, and products manufactured to speed the process, but the easiest way is probably the best.

Arrange a home for the compost heap—perhaps six by four feet, with three wooden sides of plywood boards, fixed to upright supports. The heap itself stands on bare earth, preferably open to the sun, which effectively heats the materials.

Almost anything goes into the compost pile: layers of soil alternating with salad trimmings, lawn clippings, leaves, fish trimmings, eggshells, potato peels. As this motley collection of organic waste rises in height, it should be turned repeatedly and soaked often. Seaweed is a good activator; stale beer or wine also speeds the leavening process. The nettle stings the heap into action. What goes on is a kind of fermentation; the heap becomes a varied banquet of materials.

The compost becomes a rich, dark, satisfying mass that will in turn produce new flowers and new vegetables.

May 23

May is a time of softness. There is a gentleness and a fragility to the fifth month, which is the transition time from spring to summer. Throughout the country, most of winter's dangers have passed or been averted—hard frost, windstorms; the warmed earth, softening and loosening, is on its way to the full firm ripeness of summer. Still, the sky has a tender innocent look and blossoms are evanescent and ephemeral. There is little to hold onto in May. The day, a pollen-gold spill of light, cools quickly; sudden rains or a cold spell can wipe out gardening hopes. It is too early to do much mountain exploring, and the beaches are often chilly. The "merry month" is one for mild experiences: low-country walks, feasting on fresh asparagus (a delicacy of flavor and greenness), early picnics.

Wildflowers are in friendly bloom in this delicate changing time: prairie violet, wild geranium and wild columbine exploit the possibilities of unpaved America. Scarce now, the trailing arbutus was the Pilgrim's "Mayflower"; the delicate sheen of the pink flower shines in the pine woods of the East.

Birds, building nests and hurrying to put them to use, seem unsuspicious and vulnerable; a nest is a fragile composition of earth materials and items borrowed from man. Householder English sparrows use cigarette stubs, odds and ends of anything to house the fragile eggs. Often birds are fond of white to add to their nests, what man would consider a sign of truce or peaceful intentions.

May 24

Policeman of the high mountain meadows is the hoary marmot. His life is one of dedicated attention. On duty from May to September, depending on the snows, he stands sentry in his short intense period of wakefulness: a creature grizzled with gray frosted fur and gifted with commanding eyesight and a powerful voice.

Like the groundhog, the marmot, member of the woodchuck family, is a signal of winter's end. With melting snows, he emerges from his den and takes a look around. In the spring, after his long sleep, the marmot is skimpy-thin, an unprepossessing animal. By midsummer he will be a "rich" marmot with a dignified paunch, a fat little banker guarding against winter.

First duty for the marmot: to find a mate. In about six weeks, two to five young are born. Good provider and family man, the marmot eats lavishly and with a fine aesthetic sense: grasses, roots, berries, flowering plants. He is fond of the high meadows' prettiest flowers: sky blue lupine, phlox. Strong paws with four black fingers dig out wild onions. Feasting on beauty, the marmot soon becomes supple and lustrous.

But he is vigilant in his police duty. Living in small communities, seven or more in a group, marmots may depend for safety on the one acting as sentinel. The shrill whistle means danger, and the marmots run to drop holes. If the hole is more than a few yards away, safety means a terrifying run. In grave danger, the marmot simply freezes, and waits, immobile.

His enemies: coyote, wolf, fox, and lynx. He is the prey of golden eagles. Man has been the greatest enemy; hunters often have killed marmots because of that warning whistle—heard as far as a mile—which would send deer to safety.

The piercing whistle, much like a human's, has confused hikers and climbers. In fog, one mountaineer party gamely followed a series of alarm whistles away from their route.

In national parks, marmots become accustomed to humans, and do not run at the approach of hikers. At the side of a trail, four or five marmots may be seen draped over the rocks, grey bodies matched to the stone, as calmly attentive to their surroundings as peaceful Buddhas. Through the years, these boulders will be polished smooth by successive generations of these patient sentries.

French Canadian voyageurs called him *le siffleur*—the whistler. Actually, the marmot does not move his lips or open his mouth, but forms the whistle in his throat.

Summer is short, and if a time for duty, it is a time for play, too. Lucky observers have seen marmots—both youngsters and adults—playing tag, moving with rippling agility through the grasses, cat-graceful. Then suddenly, perhaps at the arrow-shadow of an eagle in the sky, the alarm whistle blows—and the marmots have vanished again.

May 26

For Walt Whitman, May was the bumblebee month. Bumblebees, larger in size than their cousins, the honeybees, have an undeserved reputation for ferocity. Their appearance is formidable— great furry black and gold bodies, and bumblebees can hardly be said to be amiable; still, they are no warriors. Nor are they particularly organized, at least to the degree of orderly efficient bureaucracy of other insects; they live in casual villages rather than well-developed towns. Bumblebees are more given to idle rambling, early on, when the first warm days entice the bees out, and they move with a kind of stately languor across lawns and flowers, uncertainly poised between torpor and ambition. They (apparently) strike out in any direction whatever, antennae testing (just testing) the new-fragrant air.

Now in May they have shaken off lassitude, but still present a picture of next-to-confusion, moving almost at random; that is, the purpose is there but not as clearly evident as in the food-gathering swoops and dives of gulls, or the neat patterned flights of geese. Language has borrowed the movements of the bumblebee; one who bumbles is vulnerable to indecision or uneasy shifts of confidence. Bumblebees have a liking for fences, moving back and forth, searching along the posts and knots. Neither particularly well organized or peppery-tempered, they present a summer spectacle like May itself—a frank brisk activity of color and sound in their lively humming and their well-meaning activities. The bumblebee is a pageant. He might be giving a lesson in how best to enjoy life.

Old beliefs that have the habit of lingering make the bumblebee a prophet; if one flies into your house in the morning, it means good luck; a visit in the afternoon spells bad luck.

May 27

There is something in wildness that is bolder, stronger, more knowledgeable, than in the domestic. Wildness has an intimacy with earth, an adaptability that is not freedom or escape, but a compulsion of the self. Willa Cather spoke of the irregular and intimate quality of things made entirely by hand; in nature the counterpart is the wild flower, the wild plant.

The shape and color are not as standardized or dependable, seemingly, or rather, the will to breed conforms to the subtle mechanisms of original response and growth, in interaction with other living things, and hardly competes or even stands by itself. A judge of flowers or the flower show cannot separate, say, the wild rhododendron from its wet-shining forest neighbors. In late spring, the rhododendrons are in massed bloom in Washington in woods and near Hood Canal, and in Oregon in the damp foothills below Mount Hood. A town here is named for the flower, which stands in entire communities of husky glossed leaves and bright rose-lavender flowers. There is little subtlety here in the frank showy color and profusion; wild rhododendrons are a dime a dozen. Adaptable, certainly, beautiful, perhaps; but by what standards, those of the pines and firs? Do neighbors of the woods admire each other, or at least applaud the efforts of the struggling seeds? No one here to award ribbons to the rhododendron or improve on it; the color and the strength come from its own perfect interaction with acid-rich soil and dampness and cloud-streaked days.

No one owns the wild rhododendron or can take credit for it. Nature is a company of self-starters.

May 29

The human mind has need of giants. Witness the histories of the great Norse giants, of Goliath, of Paul Bunyan, and the necessary counterpart, Jack the Giantkiller. If each generation has trouble in understanding its successor, it has its immense predecessors; men were bigger "in those days."

Favorite giant, whose shadow looms large across the pages of Northwest history/legend, the Bigfoot or Sasquatch. He was seen years ago, more frequently in the 1800s, and is still glimpsed occasionally in strange disturbing sightings from early summer on—a silver shadow in the trees, monstrous footprints by a riverbank. He has been the subject of an odd movie (an erect female glancing over her shoulder as she strides into deep brush), records (the reconstructed sound of a distressingly humanoid cry), books, drawings, and some reasonably serious and respectable anthropological essays and expeditions. No one has succeeded (yet) in tranquilizing, capturing a Sasquatch and bringing him to court for appraisal and a ruling one way or the other—does he exist?

Certainly he does exist, in a manner of speaking, being more of a local than the elusive Yeti snowman, and there is a large midden of quasi-evidence and supposition and folklore and here and there a shell of fact. It is after all just possible that there is a generous-sized (700- to 800-pound) erect furred creature living in the forestlands along the Cascade chain from British Columbia to northern California. Stranger, supposedly nonexistent creatures have been discovered, and scientists worthy of the name rule out no possibilities. The creature may be (partly) humanoid—or at least a playful evolutionary intermediary between ape and man. If so, he is reduced in ranks; there could be no more than 20-30 of these big fellows, living on nuts and wild plants, shyly disappearing when humans get too close, yet frankly curious of logging trucks and machinery. Ape Canyon near Mount Saint Helens in Washington is a fitting locale for these monsters. Mood-struck and darkly brush-filled, the steep-walled canyon descends from the Plains of Abraham on the mountain's east side. In 1924, miners working there shot at one Sasquatch—they had been seeing mysterious footprints—and had the experience of having their cabin bombarded all night with boulders flung by the angry giants. Since then, a skier has vanished unaccountably (he was of course fleeing the Sasquatch) and people gaze in speculation toward the wandering lava tubes and caves.

In the 1970s campers saw the Sasquatch along the Columbia River; flyers in a small private plane north of Yosemite glimpsed a strange large creature that was of course Bigfoot. Footprints are measured and casts are made. A city law was passed in Oregon making it unlawful to shoot the Sasquatch—a reasonable gesture; if they exist, they should be studied and preserved. Certainly this is an endangered species.

Oversized bear? Hoax? Invention? (As a tourist attraction, the Sasquatch is only moderately successful; people come following a sighting, but excitement dies quickly.) Occasionally, he is seen as far east as Wisconsin, but seldom; these giants are more likely in the West, which remains in many areas relatively unmapped and inaccessible.

Almost, it is irrelevant whether or not the Sasquatch is "real." Larger than life, he broadens the mind, enlarging the spectrum of possibilities of the human landscape.

As one by one man drives away the familiar giants, the grizzly, the buffalo—shooting them or reducing them to emasculated shadows living on reservations like the saddened remnants of the Indian population—the Sasquatch fills the gap that is left, answering that need for the large, mysterious and powerful, the great somber giant of woods and canyons, and the not-so-sure-of-itself human mood.

May 30

In high country, in May, the opening meadows as the snows recede, belong to mosquitoes. In hordes large enough to smother men and horses, they strike, circular fashion, immense clouds of stalwart and hungry high-pitched voices. In a particularly bad year, hikers wrap their heads in wool and emerge from a mosquito zone gasping.

In the lower valleys, mosquitoes do not act so much in

concert, but seek out individually their victims. Less prevalent, except along marshes and riverbanks, these are hardy, anarchistic survivors.

Little to like about mosquitoes, who at their worst carry malaria or yellow fever, at best, leave welts, mildly irritating to most people, and puffy festering sores to others.

The female is mightier than the male; mosquitoes have the most effective matriarchy, since it is the female who stings and buzzes, and occurs in great numbers, being both adaptable and fecund. In most species, the females are required to be vampires. A condition of motherhood: they must suck the blood of a warm-blooded animal if the eggs are to develop.

An elaborate sequence of growth in these tiny creatures; in the genus *Calex*, for example, the female lays rafts of eggs in a convenient pond or puddle. The larvae hatch and become wrigglers, and after four separate larval stages emerge as adults. The entire sequence takes only two to three weeks.

The house mosquito—prolific and annoying—makes its small intense presence felt; an eighth of an inch long, it is bloodthirsty and accurate.

May 31

TREES AS FACTORIES

Trees spring lavishly to life in spring, putting forth entire green frothy canopies of bud and leaf; now, in full bloom and conspicuously attired in their spring garb, trees seem magical.

Photosynthesis may be another name for God; at least this complicated chemical process regulates most living things.

Trees are highly efficient converters; as factories they respond to lengthening days and the greater light and warmth, triggered to produce cambium and bark. Annual rings of growth record as neatly as any ledger the raw materials taken in, the products put forth.

These slow-growing plants work in silence, and answers are scarce to any chemical analysis of cellulose and chlorophyll. Trees that live for centuries and grow taller than most buildings begin, like everything else, with a seed. Here the mystery begins.

◇◇◇◇◇◇◇◇◇◇◇◇◇◇◇◇◇◇◇◇◇◇◇◇◇◇◇◇◇◇◇◇◇◇◇◇◇◇

June 1

A climb of a high mountain on the first of June seems early, an unconscionable adventure, for snow still covers the mountains, and muscles may not yet be used to the pull and strife of climbing. Still this is the best part of the year to climb mountains that will later be bare and rocky, the worst kind of tedious scree struggle. Now the snow is packing more firmly, making for pleasant—if slippery—walking. The world beyond the blanketed lodges and the noisy road is a blue and white world of innocent shapes and unvisited heights; the shadow of the mountain lies like a peaked hat across the ridges below. Silence on an early June dawn; only the quick squeak of snow under the boot, the climber gains a sense of virtue and of sacrifice, leaving birds behind and venturing toward the clouds.

Unseasonable cold—summer has not arrived in the mountains; the climber's breath adds to the mists. Clouds are still racing around the summit, going nowhere, trapped by lower temperatures and the solid stationary bulk of the mountain itself. With painstaking slowness the day warms itself, rocks become pink and alive in first sun. Three or four hours' steady climbing, and the climber is part of the silence and the wind-driven fog. Then, in full sun, the fog escapes, the summit is nearly there—another two or three hours away. Little record of man's visit—crampon scratches on the snow. In sacrifice, there is reconciliation; the first summit of the year is an achievement.

The summit register is still buried in ice and the view is inconsequential; but the mountain is solid beneath the feet and the sky, so close at hand, is an astonishing navy blue.

June 2

Patterns for June: sunrays repeating themselves in the petals of flowers, butterflies like petals, unfolding days.

June 3

Voice of a June twilight is the whippoorwill. Most people have heard him; not so many have seen the elusive bird, which is tireless in his call but reticent. He stands offstage, repeatedly calling his name, but hesitates to make an appearance, and early listeners mistook him for a nighthawk.

Close at hand, the bird has a rude strident sound. Almost always, a low harsh note begins the call: chuck-whip-poor-will. Further away, the sound has almost a melancholy tone, as he repeats his name over and over.

Appropriately, the scientific name is *Antrostomus vociferus*. The whippoorwill can be a bad-tempered and articulate scold; campers putting up tents in whippoorwill territory have been briskly scolded and threatened; disturbed female whippoorwills whine and hiss over supposed intrusions near the nest.

The mottled color of the leaves and branches where he perches, the whippoorwill is no vegetarian; he mostly eats large insects, and—rarely—may be seen darting open-mouthed from his perch to swallow an insect. Nesting is casual; the two eggs are simply deposited on a bed of leaves.

Why the endless calling? The twilight is heavy with the sound. Later during the night, silence, and then the bird again calls just before dawn, repeating his name in grave persistence.

June 4

Boldest pattern of June is the flower.

June 5

Wild roses, unlike their settled city cousins, are explorers. Their roots search throughout the ground for lodging; the bushes and vines themselves are tangles of gusty exuberance. Cut and brought into a house, the wild roses fade and die quickly. In contrast, roses in gardens have the showy disciplined look of fashion models. Roses—everyone's favorite—are not easy to raise, requiring pampering and pruning; much of the year they stand bare and brown. In June they come into full bloom, colored and scented with the softness of summer. Wild roses, more enterprising, have already been in bloom a few weeks.

June 6

Flower fields in bright bloom prove the scarcity of blue as a flower color. Nature is fond of blue, drenching space and expanses of sky and water with blue; the great majority of flowers are reds and yellows and pinks—warm aggressive colors that advertise the nectar (though bees show a preference for the blue-violet spectrum). Blue flowers, greatly outnumbered, are a serene minority and among the prettiest of flowers: tall delphinium, sky-colored lupine, bluebells, the brave medallions of bachelor's button, morning-cool Dutch iris, hyacinth, intensely blue wild chicory.

Blue flowers are tranquil punctuation in a garden, resting spaces between vivid companions; an all-blue garden would seem contrived and unnatural, like cold blue Christmas trees. Blue is a color to be planned for; gardeners used to put iron nails in the ground, hoping for the acid soil in which the blue hydrangea would blossom.

June 7

A certain element of risk or downright hazard is as much a part of life as being fed, or warmed, or going to sleep. Nature is taking chances all the time—the profligate seed, the gamble on the new mutation in the species, the flowers that bloom before the frost, the rabbit that ventures out in hawk-supervised brush. Only man plays the game so cautiously, weighing the chances and the probabilities, keeping a worried eye close to his own skin.

Children know instinctively that to be alive is to run a risk, and pay for growing up in cuts and scratches and bruises, and come back for more. Older bodies are soft and riddled with age, and addled with supposition, What if I fell, or the storm comes up? Risk is the hard edge of reality.

The rock climber knows this when he holds in his hand the thin difference between being and non-being; danger calculated and reduced to its least degree, controlled by will and strength, makes the heart beat faster, and the breath come mightier.

To be fully alive is to hold life in an open hand. A warm and glowing June day is a time for taking small risks, testing heart and lungs and legs against a mountain, or a rock cliff, or an ocean shore. Life is to be held, not clutched; each breathing rich moment an adventure and a winning gamble.

June 8

Where does a flower petal leave off and a butterfly begin? A white butterfly, like a curling feather, lies briefly on a petal of a daisy and is indistinguishable from the triangular pattern of the flower. Only when it moves is there a visible break between host and guest, plant and insect.

June 9

Many yards seem to grow birds as easily as flowers. Necessities for attracting birds: friendly trees, concealing bushes, a fence where birds can preen and chat, spaces of soil and lawn alive with worms and good things to eat. Many householders woo birds with well-stocked feeders and birdbaths.

For directions on building birdhouses: *Homes for Birds*, Conservation Bulletin No. 14, Revised Edition (1969), U.S. Department of the Interior. Send $.20 to Superintendent of Documents, Government Printing Office, Washington, D.C. 20402. Provide nesting materials: bits of rag, string, and twine.

Most people will shoo away stray cats, or keep their own inside, but the right kind of cat—i.e., not too quick-witted or fast-moving—may be a desirable stimulus, one that draws the birds. Birds are proud owners of territory and share a taste for jeering and ridiculing cats, flying away easily when the cat shows an inclination to climb trees. Now the garden is alive with birds: orioles, robins, blue jays; brown thrashers flank a strolling cat, appearing not alarmed, but calling the signal to other birds, telling of the interloper. The California jay often enjoys pecking cats' tails.

Birds, like every other animal, have a well-developed sense of their own being and privilege. Having found a commodious yard, they will return faithfully.

June 11

The blue jay is the dashing admiral of the skies, cocky, aggressive, a flash of braggadocio and ill will. In his resplendent blue uniform, he is one of the least popular of birds, despite his good looks. He has a well-deserved reputation for making too much noise, chasing other birds off and in general taking all too seriously the territorial imperative. Occasionally, he will plunder other birds' nests. One of the most vocal of creatures, he calls, clatters, imitates other birds, and at dawn, shouts, in a loud rasping voice. Only in the nesting season does he have the sense to keep his mouth shut; both mates are quiet, defending their nest, but ready to make a bold outcry if threatened.

In June, the fledgling jays have gotten the other end of the stick: loud squawking cries of the parents tell the young birds to start getting their own food. The message is loud and clear. Parental scoldings are a part of the jay's lively repertoire, and in turn, the young birds develop showy and ferocious voices to match their handsome coats. Family groups move about looking for nuts and insects. The blue jays have their enemies: here and there in the evergreen forests lie a scattered cluster of feathers like fallen petals; a hawk or owl has seized an unlucky jay.

June 12

BEES AS REAL ESTATE AGENTS

Bees fill the garden in June, bright-colored and active dots of light, and in company with butterflies making the garden look like one of those pointillist paintings, composed entirely of color dots. There is little freedom in the insect world; bees play assigned roles (a few are given the job of air-conditioning the home by fanning air into the hive to evaporate water from the honey). Queens become monarchs not by heredity but by diet; they are fed royal jelly. Worker bees who lick and groom the queen carry back the message that the queen lives. If the queen dies, the queen substance is gone, and the workers set about building a new queen cell. Long live the queen.

In this honeycombed apartment world of sociability and efficiency, the language is that of the dance. Dancing scouts tell in the speed of their movements and rate of abdomen-wagging the distance and location of nectar sources. This is belly-dancing with a purpose. Bees have their own dialects; the varying species and geographical races convey information in different movements and speeds.

No wax museum, the hive; when population reaches a bursting point, the queen and her followers must find a new home. (The old quarters will be taken over by new queens.)

Swarming bees on the search for new apartments gather in a dense cluster, and scouts are delegated to investigate the real estate market. Soon the scouts return, telling through the tail-wagging dance of possible new sites. Now appraisers are enlisted to inspect the possible locations.

Reports quickly start coming back; as many as a couple of dozen possible sites will be reported on and advertised to the waiting swarm. In a few days, the swarm, attentive to these dancing advertisements, will have made its choice. Other homesites will have been advertising with dwindling frequency, but the dancing agents for these yield to the decision. The choice, made on the basis of advertising, is apparently unanimous—each worker casts a vote; the queen has no more authority than the others. Royalty reigns but does not rule.

A new home is advertised not just by movements, but by the enthusiasm of the dance. A lively dance lasting several hours is prime-time ballyhoo: "This is a great spot—this hollow in the tree on the hill."

Investigators have researched the dancing bees to test the fairness of their advertising practices; in every case the advertising was found to be honest and accurate. A sluggish dance, half-hearted in its praise, tells of a so-so dwelling place. The eager enthusiastic dancers, persuading more and more followers, describe good homesites. As appraisers and agents, bees practice truth in advertising, and queen-size is an honest term.

June 14

An idle country road is an anachronism, a shadowed walk that leads back rather than forward. Walk a quiet lane now, and all the sounds are simply the sounds of insects and birds. Along the sides of the road the tawny and green weeds have taken over and the wild roses spill in untidy and careless bouquets. The gentle translucent air is filled with poignant scents: raw dirt, pungent weed blossoms.

Left to itself, a country road reverts to wildness; chuckholes made by rain and snow open, and weeds grow rapidly to fill in. In a few years, a neglected road will prosper under the ministrations of diligent nature and become once more itself—wild, tangled, and eventually impassable. While it can still be walked the road offers a cheerful lunacy, an aimless meandering; the shadowed trees casting dark-form shapes of branches look like old men leaning on their canes, sighing heavily with their memories.

June 15

Light is the one element craved by life. All species—plants, animals and man—respond to the turn and play of light. Not solely the rising temperatures in spring and early summer command growth; the process is never that simple. Even moisture, or the lack of it, is secondary; the plant world adapts. Day-length is the all-important factor in regulating the rate and cycles of growth. Light itself, to be effective, must be balanced with darkness; most plants require the interruption of dark periods as well as the bright. Inhibition and stimulus alike are the controls, a delicate and vastly complex system of processes in the green world. Evergreen trees like the Douglas fir and the Sitka spruce are demanding of light, requiring twelve to sixteen hours of day periods punctuated by darkness in order to grow. The beginning of growth itself, when the sensitive seed is triggered into activity, is a response to light.

Never simple, but an entire complex machinery of response and retreat, the role of light is obvious in the botanical world, less clearly seen in the zoological, and subtle where man is involved.

Still, light is craved by the human, as elemental a need as air itself. All of the ancients have worshipped the sun; surfriders and sunbathers today still respect that blazing symbol and reality. Even religions the most divorced from nature speak of "enlightenment" or "seeing the light." American Indians drew in shadowy caves the circle and rays of the sun.

A few researchers have suggested the role of the pineal gland—that third eye which reacts to light in conception, and possibly sex determination, and by inference, the entire mental and physical growth of the individual. Humans deprived of light become moody and querulous, morale is low on foggy or cloudy days, suicides occur in sun-deprived cities. The harsh polar environment and the punishment of the solitary cell derive their crippling power in part from lack of light.

Darkness is the space in which images form, but is itself positive; all living things are created by the interplay of dark and the light which registers the images of growth as cells rearrange themselves.

The men who wrote the Bible were right; the first thing they had God say in viewing the darkened empty void was "Let there be light."

June 17

The ladybug is considered good luck, both ecologically and sentimentally. Part of its good reputation stems from its proven ability to control aphids and other destructive insects. Imported ladybugs once saved the citrus groves of California, threatened by the harmful cushion scale insect. Called variously the lady bird, lady beetle, and ladybug, the insect was dedicated in the Middle Ages to the Virgin Mary. A scant quarter of an inch long, the bright scarlet beetle, black-dotted, resembles a neat ladylike breastpin. Females lay their eggs on plants infested with aphids and scale insects, insuring a good food supply for the hatching larvae.

Alighting by chance on a human hand or arm, the ladybug seems hardly disturbed, merely pausing to take its bearings; such a visit is reputed to be lucky. Another indicator of fortune: count the number of spots on a hibernating ladybug's back and you'll get that many dollars.

June 18

June heralds the return of the monarch butterfly. It has spent the winter in the more agreeable parts of the country, California and the

South, where it has migrated in groups of hundreds, now to come back in solitary impatient flight. Destination: the milkweed; this is the plant where the eggs are usually laid. Eating, growing, repeatedly molting, the caterpillar then lies like a princess on a silken mat of its own weaving, and lying there, gradually sheds its adolescent skin, becoming an odd-looking top-heavy creature.

Slowly the new outer skin hardens into a distinct covering and the insect begins its nesting stage as a chrysalis. Now it lives in a "green house with golden nails" awaiting its emergence as an adult butterfly. The house is translucent, a vivid turquoise green, and slowly the markings of the butterfly become visible through its thin walls. In twelve days the cells have reorganized and the great butterfly emerges, a handsome insect stately in its flight, as befits royalty.

June 19

In 1889 the Portland Rose Society in Oregon arranged its first exhibition. Decorated carriages, bicycles and automobiles moved slowly through the streets. The four autos proceeded so slowly and haltingly that they were jeered, and ridiculed in newspaper accounts. Since June 1907 the annual parade has been more successful. Floats from various states compete, elaborate confections of pretty girls and roses. The flowers flourish in Portland's mild, moist climate; some of the old homes in the hills overlooking the city are splendidly awash in bright gardens in June. The city of roses lives up to its name.

June 21

Now the flower fields in Lompoc, California come into full bloom. Tourists driving toward the hills roll their windows down to get a heady whiff of fragrance. Striped fields alternate in pure firm bands of color: blue delphinium, orange and bright yellow marigolds, sweetpeas in pink and lavender, crystalline white alyssum, scarlet petunias. Without a doubt the most beautiful industry in the world.

Everywhere the geraniums, casual and randomly planted in yards and side streets, pinks and reds, and the iridescent pelargoniums that borrow sea colors, and wild geraniums growing as free side-attractions to the cultivated fields.

The wind is faithful in Lompoc, and cool ocean fogs gray the mornings, beneficial to the flowers, but also causing complications. Wind carries unwanted stray seeds (most lawns in Lompoc look ragged and weedy with a stubborn, faintly dissolute appearance) and too much fog, lying heavily for a day or two in the valley, despite its pussy willow warmth, can dampen and inhibit flower bloom.

Flower growers use highly sophisticated technology to encourage new varieties and foster healthy seeds: cortisone to atomic energy. Since 1953 a seed company offered $10,000 to anyone developing a pure white marigold 2½ inches in diameter. This is finally believed to have been found.

During Lompoc's flower festival—an ambitious celebration for this minuscule town—there are parades, art shows, and formal judging of bouquets and arrangements, all to celebrate man's growing and production of flower seed.

No one seems to realize this is absurd.

June 22

SUMMER BEGINS

The days are as long as they will ever be. Even clouds and sea have lost their chill under the generous long spread of light. Officially the first day of summer marks the new season, and on a mild June day, summer seems young, still holding out infinite promise; yet tomorrow the swing will start back, the days will be starting to shorten again. In a sense the first day of summer is also its last.

June 23

Nature, too, has its missionaries. They spread the gospel of light and air and tree scents.

In itself, nature seems too harsh, too external, too rude a habitat for man, who has always fled from the natural world or attempted to control it by breaking the sod, cutting away the trees, paving the land. People used to believe mountains were populated with dragons and ogres; mountains were seen as ugly distortions of nature, crude excrescences of shapes festering like old wounds. The raw materials of nature were there to be converted into cash; early settlers broodingly looked on the forests as so many board feet of lumber.

Civilization has always been man against nature; it has been considered a proof of mental and moral advancement to strip the habitat and domesticate its population. Early church fathers held that cruelty to animals was bad not because it hurt the animals, but because it might lead to cruelty against other men. As a species, man has always pitted himself against his world. The American Indians were savages to the civilized eye simply because they accepted nature and did not quarrel with it or capitalize on it.

Still, a few missionaries spread the word of the beauty and meanings of nature. Walt Whitman, reveling in the sensuous delight of woods and flowers, spoke for what is restless and unsatisfied in man—a nobler greed. John Muir was successful—"Thus I pressed Yosemite upon him like a missionary offering the gospel"—because he overthrew the barriers. Himself the product of a dour Calvinist background, where all the woods and streams incited to wildness and shamelessness, Muir was a joyous rambler who lived his own message of light and serenity, trusting wholeheartedly in nature itself as transcendent experience. In later years, he went further and further from conventional thought, seeing God or that consciousness which was a reasonable facsimile in stone and forest; his defeat in the fight to save the Hetch-Hetchy Valley left him weakened and despairing.

Of the modern-day missionaries, David Brower has been the most spectacular success—and failure. Called the Archdruid, Brower was the loud angry voice of the Sierra Club, demanding equal rights for nature and urging on man the concept of himself as one part only in a complex world. Missionaries are not generally well liked or tolerated if they demand too many unreasonable sacrifices, offering their listeners the unpalatable tasks of contrition and obedience. Brower was ousted (excommunicated is perhaps the word); like Muir he stepped on too many loggers' and miners' toes. Of late, missionaries are considered fanatics; environmentalists are unsensible radicals in their caves, nature is threat rather than promise, in the wild firmness of unchanging patterns and cycles, an insult rather than blessing.

Having ousted himself from heaven, man considers it a place to visit, not to live.

June 24

Gross old man of a June evening is the bullfrog, croaking in solitary splendor on the lily pad or stump he has claimed as his territory. Large, yellow-green-mottled, he requires only a cigar and a tophat to reenact his role of impresario. The mellow bass voice carries over the countryside.

Breeding begins in June in northern areas, considerably earlier in the South as the air and water warms. Lover of the summer night, the concert baritone produces black and white eggs that float in surface slime. These will become 4- to 6-inch tadpoles, and later the 3½-inch to 8-inch adults. Some listeners hear in the deep croak a thirst for more than love; the bullfrog is calling for a bottle of rum.

June 26

June is for strawberries. Wild strawberries bloom along the roads that climb toward wooded foothills; strawberries move in leaping growth from beds and unwind from strawberry barrels. Red, juice-bursting, freckled as a summer's face, the berries are the fruit of June; in actuality not a berry, but an aggregate fruit, bearing seeds which are a kind of small fruit on the surface.

Gardeners plant lettuce and strawberries together for companionable growth; some, harking back to a truthful old wives' tale, mulch the berries with pine needles, and lay bits of twig and random cones on the bed. Strawberries seem to respond to the tangy smell.

In places like Oregon's lush and fertile Willamette Valley, a green basin of ripeness becomes a giant strawberry bowl.

Strawberries are for eating out of hand (let the juices spill) and for the traditional feast of shortcake, which can stand as a supper in itself:

2 c flour	*1 t sugar*
1 t salt	*5 T shortening*
4 t baking powder	*Milk*

Sift together dry ingredients and work in the shortening. Just enough milk is added to make a soft dough. Form into six generous shortcakes, place on greased cooky sheet, and bake at 425° for 10-12 minutes, till crusty and golden. No whipped cream for true strawberry lovers, who split and butter the shortcake and fill to heaping with crushed and sweetened berries.

June 27

June occurs throughout the country in a blissful democracy; some states will be a little slower in responding to light, a little cooler, but first summer is a benison, bestowed with regularity in lengthening days and even, gentle warmth. A few chilly places in the Northwest lag behind; in Seattle, a standard joke: "Hope summer comes on a weekend this year."

May—fickle and still a little delicate—was considered by the Romans to be bad luck for weddings; traditionally, the more settled, ripening June is bride's weather. It is weather fit for a queen; England observes the royal birthday in June. Birds are sociable, sweet in their singing, and gentle-voiced. A placidity in gardens, where flowers stir leisurely under the sun. A day in June is not rare, but has a common quality everywhere: its mildness.

June 28

Now the snows are gone from the lower elevations of Sequoia National Park in California and the immense trees stand fully open and revealed. Having survived the snows, now the trees will live through the dry hot summer. The size is deceptive: at first approach the trees seem relatively ordinary, a somewhat larger than average tree; it is only when a human goes to stand by one of these giants that he suspects the enormity—and the age—of the tree.

Tall as a twenty-five-story building, the trees have trunks that may measure thirty feet across. Thirty-two persons have danced on the stump of a sequoia. Largest is the General Sherman tree—biggest tree in the world at 272.4 feet in height and 101.6 feet around. Weighing 625 tons, it stands impassive in mountain winds.

It takes a good deal to kill a sequoia; these trees were young and vigorous 2,000 years before Christ was born, they were middle-aged when Columbus discovered America, and they still stand—survivors of fire, erosion, and wind. The true enemy is man, who were noisy giantkillers, slaughtering hundreds of the trees in the 1800s, to exhibit split and reassembled stumps at world fairs, and hurrying to build a sawmill nine miles from the Giant Forest. Man seems not particularly awed by age and size, but threatened by the mystery.

In 1852, a hunter named A. T. Dowd had come running into camp, boasting: "Killed the biggest grizzly bear that I ever saw in my life." No one had believed his story of incredibly tall trees but they were willing to follow him to inspect a giant grizzly. Now they gaped at the biggest tree they had ever seen, and Dowd asked confidently, "Do you still think it's a yarn?" They believed; other people came to laugh and were amazed, and set about looking for profit in these astonishing creations. Trees could be exhibited after a fashion; the brittle wood is useless for building.

Later, in 1858, Hale Thorp, cattle stockman, less ambitious to be a logger, followed two Indians to discover the Giant Forest, and then set up housekeeping in a hollow sequoia log. Here he lived, at the edge of tranquil meadows, in his centuries-old house, small but ship-snug, entertaining among his guests John Muir, who found the setting of the hospitable tree-cabin piquant.

Appropriately the tree is named for that remarkable Cherokee Indian, Sequoyah, whose accomplishments included inventing an alphabet, and whose name means "neither this nor that." Neither this forest fire not that lightning ordinarily bothers much the indomitable sequoia.

The bark is the color of summer: flushed and warm, a living vibrant red. Older trees carry the scars of their long lives. Resting on shallow roots which go barely an arm's length into the soil, the trees send these roots as far as 400 feet to search out food from the soil.

Sequoias begin life as a seed the size of a pinhead. Millions of these seeds are flung out in nature's customary extravagance but only a rare seed takes hold and begins the long march upward. At the age of 100, the sequoia is a mere adolescent stripling—150 feet tall and 6 feet in diameter.

Not until 1890 did President Harrison sign the bill establishing Sequoia National Park, giving belated protection to the Big Tree— variously called Sierra redwood or *Sequoiadendron giganteum*.

Visitors drive through hollowed-out tunnel trunks, gape up at the reaching height, clamber onto a fallen giant to touch the moist rosy bark.

The trees are silent, in their shade sheltering the lively and vocal squirrel, raccoon and chipmunks. John Muir spoke of the "auld lang syne" of trees; certainly there are enormous memories standing here, and yet the trees have still a look of waiting.

June 29

The blackened dead lava of ancient volcanoes seems an unlikely arena for the adventure of life, and in fact it does take a while, but the imperative of nature is growth. Where lava spilled and ran in fierce hot tongues, burning everything in sight, it hardens into tortuous ankle-breaking masses; now in June wild flowers appear here and there. Perched against charcoal-colored tangles, a stray *Lupinus volcanicus*, bright blue. Climbers wrestling with the crumbly rock walls of old volcanic pinnacles like Three-fingered Jack in Oregon reach for a hand-hold and touch a stray sedum, or stonecrop. The wrinkled pumice slopes of Mount Saint Helens in Washington—a comparatively young volcano as volcanoes go—slowly are beginning to support life once more. Dry rock is in truth a desert; such tiny flowers, economical of moisture, are the most tenacious of prospectors staking out a claim.

Cataclysms have their role to play in the shifting and rearranging of life patterns. A volcanic eruption seems the most abrupt and brutal of disasters. If Mount Rainier were to erupt again (and scientists are measuring the occasional escaping steam hisses of this giant teakettle), houses and farms and people would be so much kindling; yet the volcanic ash, broken down by weather, deposits a rich bounty of minerals in the soil. Only nitrogen is lacking.

The cooling lava can even produce patterns of beauty in itself. Lava that cools abruptly becomes obsidian, the bright transparent black of the glass mountains of Oregon and California. The glass is harder than window glass. Actually, obsidian is colorless, appearing black because of minute dust particles. In some varieties the tiny unformed crystals are red or brown.

Indians gathered and traded for this rock to make glittering arrow points. Occasionally the obsidian, cooling and combining with other matter, produces delicate and intricate patterns of white, the gemlike snowflake obsidian.

June 30

All of nature is alive, conscious and moving. It is impossible to walk in a garden, in the woods, along a beach, down a country road, or to the summit of a mountain, and escape this fact. Humming of insects like the wind itself, flash of color in a flower as a butterfly moves; it strikes and leaps and gambols from all sides—the dance of the cells. Life like time is a dense multilayered level of vibration, both horizontal and linear. Everywhere the straining movement toward light, the ripening; yet already the seed is in the fruit, and the fruit in the seed—the pattern unfolds even in the making of the new pattern.

Bees have (perhaps) a shared consciousness, snatched in flight with another groping bee; the ants know in their cells what another ant is feeling, if feeling is defined not as a subjective message from cell to cell within one body but across and through the shapes of like cells. Plants have a dim and relaxed low-key consciousness; seemingly idle and at ease, they take life as it comes in the warm sunlight, without any apparent thought. Yet immense planning is there in the green, carefully constructed stalks, and a convoluted blossom seems an example of perfect knowledge. Consider the lilies of the field! is not so much an exhortation to idleness as a command to be alive and economical in every cell, aware of one's destiny in every pore. Birds describe a winged dance toward their nests, both succor and entreaty; the young birds will soon be flying. A coyote and her stilt-legged pups, moving across the edge of the woods, is perfect example of mind at work: instruction and love (of a sort), the more selfless love because she is teaching the pups what she herself learned, the fullness and chance and choices of life.

A man considers himself to be product of nature's highest consciousness, or sometimes an apart and separate consciousness, coldly observing as on a screen the complex chase of life. A century after Darwin, men who accepted evolution still believed themselves somehow the crown of that sly process.

Yet man is at his most alive—his most conscious—when he simply watches and lets the patterns and the movement and sound dart and dance into and share his own mind. The seeing eye is also part of the game; man is witness and participant in the myriad becomings.

Rocks are generally considered to be inanimate, lifeless, the other end of the scale. Yet rocks, in themselves lifeless, are possibly stored-up life, the far rim of the circle, in total abandon to the processes of glacier or rain or decay. Stored organic matter becomes a form of rocks, and life started in fragments drifting from stone stars. Each species—each pattern—has a time scale; rocks simply live longer, and at a slower pace. Impossible always to ascribe a purpose to nature's processes, purpose is an arbitrary definition to sort out things for man's befuddled brain; yet nature is indisputably active—and the activity never stops.

Summer:
Bounteous Noon

July 1

The essence of July is sweetness: honeysuckle, clover, the scent of columbine as it wraps itself around a porch, roses climbing a fence, smell of grass at newest dawn, red raspberries. Scents mingle in the air but seem as individual and familiar as mating scents to bees and butterflies. (Some male butterflies themselves possess scales that are scent organs, secreting a fluid said to attract females.) Clover is clever, claiming and rebuilding the soil wherever it gets the chance; on the other hand, bees need clover in order to stake out their own life rights. Aphids secrete honeydew, the sweetish liquid much coveted by bees, wasps, and ants. Some species of ants adopt aphids as their cows to ensure a steady supply.

The spicy pepper bush and the buttonbush with its jasminelike fragrance scent the air and attract nectar-eager insects. Wild flowers are in July as prolific as the visiting butterflies, with a showy vigor decorating the landscape, stronger and more confident than the first delicate ornaments of spring. The blue chicory opens to the sunshine, jewelweed sparkles like earrings, dayflower is a morning bloom, pickerelweed offers its succession of brief-living blossoms, sweetbrier adorns fields and thickets. Meadowsweet raises its tiny pyramids of pink and white blossoms.

July 2

Patterns for July: seed cells, faceted pine cones, the neat rows of corn kernels, lichen-speckled rocks, the elaborate jewel and machinery patterns of insects, stars flung casually and at random in the sky.

July 3

Dog days begin. Romans called the six or eight hottest weeks of the summer *caniculares dies*. They believed the dog star Sirius rose with the sun and added to the heat; therefore the days of July and August got a double measure of heat, from both the sun and the dog star.

July 4

Fireflies are nature's fireworks. The bright tiny lanterns swing and dance in the warm evenings. Warning? Beacon? Signal? No one knows for sure; species of fireflies that do not glow seem able to survive and prosper as well as their luminous cousins. Researchers have attempted to prove, not too successfully, that the flashing light is linked to mating; other theories hold that the light is a caution signal (most birds will not dine on fireflies).

Males of one species inhabit treetops and flash a chilly turquoise light a few times; females like a claque sit on the ground and respond with a few twinkling flashes. A common species is *Photinus marginellus*, flashing yellow just at the end of twilight and stopping when complete darkness comes, though a few persistent fireflies flash on into the night. Odd and magical-seeming, like falling stars, the fireflies seem as pointlessly beautiful as a Japanese painting, merry as Gilbert and Sullivan performers.

July 5

Nature's apartment dwellers live in trees. The brown pinecones are ripening on branches; generous accommodations for the future generations, the seeds maturing here.

The trees themselves are impressive—ponderous was the word first given to ponderosa pine—and pine trees are vulnerable to too many uses; early vast stands of the eastern white pine were virtually wiped out by loggers. The cone itself carries the secrets, like a package with instructions for opening and delivery. When the cone matures, it turns down, the scales open, and the winged seeds are carried away by the wind. A pinecone picked up from the ground is scaly and firm, each guard set as precise as a shingle; warm from the soil, it seems complete in itself, a creature with shape and living cells.

July 6

Farmers used to pray to a merciful Providence; the first pioneers to come West looked for the inescapable bounty of the land, green and lush beyond the paper-dry deserts and the unwelcoming barrier of the mountains. Even in an age of machinery and atomic energy a residual belief clings, a knee-jerk of hope or faith: the idea of the watchmaker inherent in the watch, the feeling that there must be a provider since there are provisions. In part this explains the natural stubborn feeling of ill will toward farmers' subsidies; nature should somehow provide for us. To have to pay, at times outrageously, for the stuff that springs from the land, seems confusing and illogical. The concept of farming itself—and every year hundreds of people "return" hopefully to the land in the hopes of a simple, self-sufficient life—means to attach oneself to the soil, and seize what will be provided.

The mercy and bounty of the harvest is implicit in the green and tawny hayfields of July, the ripening corn and fruits, the dance of flowers intermingled with the strict productive rows of vegetables. After a fashion, nature is providence, but providence has its other side: the sudden brief storm in July that flattens the cornfield and leaves the parading tassels lying like so many besmirched Shriners' hats, the woodchuck that comes along and eats the squash. The truth of nature's providence is excess, the prodigal father.

An unaccountable generosity (of a sort) tosses millions of sequoia seeds on the ground and one (maybe) will take hold. Insects in every size and shape when a few varieties seemingly would have been enough. Spendthrift seeds of every living thing including man's sperm in such a grotesque excess beyond provision that only the tiniest minority make it, almost oddities instead of probabilities. Hordes of wild flowers blooming in crowded oversupply. Last May the blossoms of apricots like popcorn on the branches; now a few fruit, what remains after rain, wind, inquiring birds, voracious insects. Nature is like a person working in the dark, making 500 copies of everything in the vague hope one will survive. The balance of ecology is overproduction and overpopulation. In the face of such mindless activity, it seems ridiculous and idealistic to talk of conservation; the essence of nature's providence is waste.

July 9

DECORATING THE AIR

A jeweled hatpin stabs at a flower. Vibrating in the air, a tiny hummingbird looks like an aerial ornament; when the sun catches its throat as it makes a quarter-turn, the color is iridescent green. This is a male hummingbird, dressed like a miniature courtier.

Early naturalists attempted to press hummingbird bodies, much in the manner of botanical specimens. At one time, thousands of the tiny birds were slaughtered to make ornaments for ladies' hats; probably entire species were wiped out in this quest for feathered jewelry. Hummingbirds have been considered oversize bees. Brazilians call the little bird *beija-flor*—"kiss-flower."

A bird so tiny—weighing about the same as a penny—can claim a number of large accomplishments: he can fly upside down or backwards or sideways, he can on occasion attain the speed of 30-40 miles per hour, he can fly nonstop up to 500 miles in migration. He lives high and fast, a terrific concentration of rapid bonfire metabolism and nervous aggressive seeking. He seems to live in a perpetual rapture of excitement. To gain the energy for these feats, he eats a prodigious quantity of food—nectar and protein in insects—proportionately the same quantity as a man eating 300 pounds of food a day. Does he burn himself out fast, living at this astonishing rate? Not at all; hummingbirds have been known to live at least seven to nine years.

Red is his color, in flowers and at his throat. The ruby-throated hummingbird is the common species in eastern America; in July that blazing flash and glimmer of red is a familiar color. Species of flowers, in turn, have evolved accommodatingly to provide nectar (often scentless, no lure for insects) on tubelike or trumpet-shaped sources, borne in exposed, open inflorescences where the hummingbird can hover without striking its wings on leaves, twigs, or the protruding lip of other flowers which bees and butterflies use for a landing platform.

The nest is tiny, a mere thimble size, an inch deep, often with a lip or rim that helps keep the young birds safely inside. Daintily crocheted together with cobwebs, such a nest may pass for a knot on a tree.

Darting and buzzing with a nervous accuracy at bright-colored flowers, the bird exhibits a fussy, can't-sit-still liveliness. Hummingbirds are inquisitive; in high country they buzz hikers' caps and jackets, and often exhibit a flashy courage, impudently chasing birds five times their size.

Not particularly a sociable bird—and male hummingbirds take no part in raising the young—the hummingbird has on occasion seemed to recognize humans, or displays an often lively impatience, fussing about a person hanging a feeder from a garden tree limb.

A flash in the air, a blurring vibration for a few seconds, the flash of gem colors, and the bird flies off. In a burst of playful exuberance, he may simply swing in the air—a giddy hummingbird on an invisible trapeze.

July 10

Rocks can serve in the garden as cover and mulch. A layer of rocks spread between plants keeps weeds down, and light porous rocks, perhaps brought from the ocean beach, will gradually disintegrate and feed the soil with minerals.

July 11

Elderberry bushes are richly in bloom along country roads. Relegated now to the weed category, the elderberry is an excessively sweet fruit, tricky for jellymaking, and retains long memories of sweetness in the old-fashioned elderberry wine:

3 lb fresh elderberries	*1 ½ qt sugar*
1 ¼ gal boiling water	*Juice 1 lg lemon*

Yeast (Early on, people did not bother with yeast. Results were therefore often unpredictable. Use a good burgundy yeast.)

Nutrient

Stem and wash the elderberries. Pour boiling water over and leave to soak for four days. Strain berries and press out juice. Add sugar, lemon juice, yeast and nutrient. Ferment to dryness. Rack and store. The wine will be fully mature in a couple of years.

Serve to: clergymen, old ladies, returned travelers—anyone who happens along.

July 12

Henry David Thoreau was born July 12, 1817. He was a disarming naturalist who was also a social critic, from the calm refuge of Walden raising a sharply dissenting voice.

Evolving from nature poet to scientific observer—committed to the true and lean account—he is remembered best now for his observations not on society, nor strictly on nature's forms and creations, but a philosophy or message that he managed to impart in phrases that reverberate with meaning: "In wildness is the preservation of the world."

Thoreau would perhaps be astonished to see today the young and the not-so-young who have found in that austere message rich meanings for their own lives. A well-bred man of developed literary tastes and well-educated colleagues, Thoreau speaks for the ragged, wandering lovers of brooks and trees, those an earlier generation called shiftless and are now called uncommitted. Like Muir, Thoreau is spokesman for the wilderness and its intermediary; it is possible to see in both men a philosophy that neither denigrates the human spirit nor makes of the wilds a pretty and sentimental backdrop. As civilization erodes the cliffs, these two solitary grand figures remain etched on the rocks.

Thoreau was perhaps the first nature writer to articulate clearly the growing realization that no bill of divorcement was written between man and nature: all of nature is one piece and man only one of its manifestations. Other earlier writers never quite voiced this realization: Isaak Walton "lovingly" attached the hook to the fish; yet Thoreau could write without embarrassment of his "fishy friend" in the pond. In a spare, nervous style, almost coolly astringent, he brought to the surface what men were beginning to sense, and showed them the obverse of the two-sided coin, the deep untapped richness of the free natural world and that part of it living in man. Objective, unemotional (on the surface), these angular writings are seemingly all thought. Actually, a passion shines through for the transcendent, the reality and *livingness* of alive nature.

July 13

SPIDERS AS BUREAUCRATS

The spider is the original organization man. Given the corner of a fence or a window, the spider sets to work with speed and efficiency, carefully laying the cables and guy wires and conforming always to angles and flat planes, and stepping around neatly and briskly to chart and construct his web. All eight legs busy, he plots the wheel, lays out the taut spokes, ever mindful to consider both tension and location. Not always are these webs precisely geometrical; the spider seems more to plan and construct as he goes along—a day-to-day problem solver with ingenuity, managing his ritualistic business.

The building of a web is a highly technical industry, and the skillful spider accomplishes it well. Once the web is constructed, it is his all-powerful organization, complex and undeviating, product of a hundred minute rules. There are no loopholes. Any break or nonconforming tear is swiftly mended.

At the very apex of the hierarchy sits the spider, upside-down. At ease in this position, hind legs extending straight behind him to support him in the center of the web, he waits, with the rest of his legs free to seize and grapple with whatever comes his way.

The web, cleverly built, is his domain, and to its stifling circumference comes the fly; the web has been organized with deadly accuracy.

July 14

A benign prairie fire blazes in mid-July in the fields and mountain meadows and prairies—the Indian paintbrush. With leaves looking very much as if they had been dipped in scarlet paint, this is a conspicuous herb—but difficult to pin down; species are many and vary in color from the attention-getting reds to white, dusty old rose, orange, faded purple. Habitat seems to change with the climate and other factors; a meadow vivid with paintbrush one season may be sparse the next. The actual flower itself is unobtrusive, an unprepossessing greenish yellow. In part, the paintbrush is parasitic, deriving nourishment from other plants such as grass roots.

A short-stemmed paintbrush found only at high altitudes is *Castilleja rupicola*, the cliff-dwelling plant with brilliant bracts and dark-red leaves, both blunt-lobed, proof of summer for venturesome hikers.

July 15

Tomatoes, fat and glossy red globes, ripen to soft sweetness on stampeding vines. The deceptive fruit was once called a love apple. Botanically, the tomato is a berry, enclosing its seeds in the fleshy bundle.

Tomatoes are summertime food: sliced and heaped on platters of cold cuts and potato salad, in thick chunks between bread for a homely sandwich, to be fried and eaten at breakfast along with eggs (with a nod to the British).

A good summer crop can climb tall fences, overrun kitchens, and set women to work canning in haste. A good tomato is as red as a patriot's July, firm as an honest handshake, as uncomplicated as a summer day.

July 16

The cool of the morning is a transient one, a tempered glow. Soon the day will build to its climax, the direct immediate heat of July. The sun, high in the sky, now sends its rays directly down. As the sea is warmer, skies may be cloudier—and wetter; occasionally a thunderstorm will break in late afternoon. Briefly, a shower: clouds are scattered and the eastern sky is brilliant-colored. Twilight comes earlier. A month after the summer solstice, days are tightened, drawing in, and bird songs are quieter; the urgent ecstatic sound of mating is already passed.

July 17

Old snow in the mountains has been acted on by rain and wind and temperature, and becomes a hardened layer. Thawing during the day, then freezing at night, snow settles into a pock-marked surface, the shallow irregular craters of sun dishes. The innocent-looking, potentially lethal cornices of spring are gone, that once leaped over the prows of hills like waves. Wind is the most lively mechanism of nature; hard-blowing wind across a snow slope will pack the snow into deeper sun dishes and often eventually into deep narrow cups intersected by columns of snow standing between the hollows. This is penitent snow, the *nieve penitentes* of high altitude that suggests praying figures and indeed makes for excessively tiresome and remorseful walking. Sometimes— near the summit of Mount Shasta, for example—there will be an entire slope or field of these unbending frozen pillars.

Snow slopes often turn a dirty reddish pink; this is the presence of the tiny snow algae. Hikers who enjoy eating snow lose their thirst when told they are eating worms—as some long-time mountaineers will (smilingly) warn novices.

Few environments present so lifeless and unwelcoming a scene as an old glacier or snowfield; yet a climber, struggling upward with his eyes downcast, sees a variety of tiny life processes: a spider follows a chilly track. Crows call near old volcanic cauldrons and butterflies float amiably on the wind currents where no flowers bloom.

July 18

Corn is the most American of American food. Entire countryman reputations have been built on fine upstanding rows of tall

silk-feathered corn. Serving fresh sweet corn is a fisherman's strike—
grab it at its melting peak of sweetness, hurriedly shuck it, drop it into
boiling water and almost at once pull it out again; heap the yellow tender
kernels with salt and butter. Even the eating of corn is a homely satisfying process, unabashed and best accomplished with vigor and not too
much fussy attention toward dripping butter or sticky fingers. Nomination for silliest invention: the fancy corn-ear holders. Corn has never
been and is not a gourmet food.

July 19

Entire meadows of wild flowers now bloom in the high
country, vast communities of flowers. Against a glacier-clad mountain,
stern and imposing in its rock/snow blueness of July, a frivolous city:
white heather, red heather, valerian, lupine, paintbrush, mountain
dock, arnica, shiny buttercup. Flowers born to bloom unseen. For every
meadow visited by photographers and tourists, there are thousands
more hidden away in high cirques no one will visit. Most meadow plants
will be eaten by small animals—many of them also never to be seen. The
pika, or cony, a diminutive rodent with soprano squeak, lives in
rockslides and is a provident harvester, clipping virtually any plant and
neatly piling it under the rocks to dry, his hay for winter.

July 20

Rocks, lying on a beach or along a trail, slowly take on the
heat of the sun and become warm to the touch. By late July, many of the
rocks that were slippery and damp with moss along watercourses have
become dry and harsh; kindling-brown lichen is a beard. Fewer rocks
cast up on the beaches these calmer days, and in the mountains, rocks
have slid and slipped downhill with the melting snows. Rock can have
an astonishing hard permanence—granite—or be the most crumbly of
crumbs of rotten scree and pumice.
All textures, all sizes, shapes, colors, and forms, rocks are

more abundant than insects, have more staying power than man. Under the pressure of traveling rivers, rocks are no more than baggage, pebbles worn smooth and round; entire rock cliffs sag slowly over the years to tumble in the ocean. Nature is continually pushing things downhill. Written on by water and vegetation, rocks carry the graffiti of time. In a field, a plough-scarred stone lies next to the fragment of an arrowhead. Most rocks are as prolific as weeds and therefore never noticed; some are sparkling or colored, and are thus considered gems. Even the most useless rock has its purposes: to carry in the pocket and roll between the fingers, to skip across a river or a lake. Yet a barren rock could produce a forest: on that gray sterility the lichen grows which feeds the moss and fern which enrich the soil which in turn nourishes the seeds of trees. Rocks in silent abundance appear the castings from which life was formed.

July 21

Great tall flowers, yellow-rayed as the sun and with a sturdy rustic look, bloom alongside the fences of Kansas and the Midwest, always facing expectantly toward the sun; the entire stem turns, continually exposing leaf surfaces to sunlight.

As a wild plant, the sunflower grows from Minnesota south to Oklahoma and Texas and west to the Pacific in sunny areas, fewer in the East. The seeds, long useful for birds, have been discovered by humans. Now many people grow the sunflower. The cultivated flower may grow to fifteen feet—five feet taller than its wild neighbor—and boast a flowering head of twelve inches diameter or more.

Sunflowers suggest old farmhouses, shady porches, the cool drink of well water, dogs drowsing in the heat of the afternoon, the fields growing pell-mell to maturity; warm memories that will nourish the bones of winter-ailing folk.

July 22

Good trail food for a hike in forests and mountains: beef jerky, hard cheese, nuts, raisins, sunflower seeds, hard candy (sometimes); sour balls are refreshing. Dry, seedy savories may be combined, often called gorp.

Thoughtful hikers equip themselves with pockets and bagfuls of provisions and nibble as continuously as squirrels.

July 24

Good books to read on backpacking:

Angier, Bradford. *Home in Your Pack*. Macmillan, 1965.
Almost any of the books by this wise and delightful writer contain helpful tips for traveling through the backcountry in comfort.

Fletcher, Colin. *The Complete Walker*. Rev. ed. Knopf, 1974.
Fletcher is the backpacker's writer. Not a how-to, but a this-is-how-I-do-it, witty, candid and infectious. Walking across the desert or negotiating the Grand Canyon, Fletcher has the spirit of walking planted firmly in his soul and feet. He is independent, an individualist willing to participate fully in nature, totally at ease with his environment much as a plant moving in the wind, and somehow able to communicate all this.

Manning, Harvey. *Backpacking; One Step at a Time*. REI, 1973.
Complete and authoritative. Ideas and suggestions for novices, family campers, and seasoned hikers, from a knowledgeable writer and climber associated with the Seattle Mountaineers.

Mohney, Russ. *The Master Backpacker*. Stackpole, 1976.
Encyclopedic in its scope and authoritativeness, the book is written in a chatty style and carries its learning lightly. The pointers contained herein are applicable to all types of terrain.

Saijo, Albert. *The Backpacker*. 101 Productions, 1974.
In gentle text and drawings, the philosophy of the outback.

Sierra Club Wilderness Handbook. Ballantine, 1971.
Authoritative, as would be expected from this large and informed organization.

July 25

Lively inhabitant of a mountain stream is the water ouzel, the bird that pretends to be a fish.

The little dipper is as much at ease underwater as on land or in the air. Using partly opened wings to push himself along, the bird moves in the stream, pecking and searching between and under rocks for food: water insects, worms, fish eggs, snails. For his underwater life the ouzel is well equipped with a thick down layer under outer feathers and a large preening gland which supplies waterproofing oil. When he dives, two tiny flaps drop over the nostrils to keep water out, and third eyelids—nictitating membranes—keep water out of the eyes.

Dipping, bobbing, dancing along the stream, each cold splash of water covering his gray body, the bird seems inarguably enjoying himself. He alights on a rock, looking something like a clumsy wren with large-footed heavy body and pert upstanding tail, and sings—a liquid chirp; then darts again in the water, unmistakably vivacious and graceful.

Water bird from the beginning: the nest is built in the crack of a moist log or even behind a waterfall, hidden from predator birds by the spray curtain. Looking like an upside-down basket, the nest is woven of grass and moss. From the four to six white eggs will emerge the little dippers, at home in the iciest, purest, tumbling mountain stream.

July 27

The meadowsides are sweet with hay.

—"Midsummer" by John T. Trowbridge

Green hay ripens to golden under the direct fast heat of July. In the Midwest, in the haying season, farmers would enjoy switchel, still a refreshing drink:

1 c light brown sugar	*¾ c white vinegar*
½ t ground ginger	*1 qt cold water*
1 c light molasses	*1 to 2 t baking soda*

Mix sugar, ginger, molasses, and vinegar. Dissolve soda in ¼ cup of the water and add. Stir into cold water. A drink that has snap, crackle, and fizz to it.

July 28

The mountain burro is a strong hiker, a (sometimes) willing companion, a carrier of fair-sized loads. As a member of a camping party he is a vocal and opinionated character. Many families include him invariably in their trips; others, having tried to coax a sulking burro up the trail, write him off as a beast of stubbornly bad disposition. More persnickety than horses, and more talkative, the burro swings its big ears to catch unfamiliar sounds, and to the peace of a mountain meadow adds his own abrupt chuckling bray.

Thoughtful-eyed, he can register in expressive face and ears the most profound disapproval of the entire trip and its members, yet proceed, fully weighted down with his load, in a sure-footed and dependable manner.

The burro is an early riser. At a chilly four-thirty or five in the morning he announces reveille to the sleeping residents of tents.

July 29

Wise old mountaineers routinely carry the ten essentials—on short hikes as well as big climbs. The practice is part common sense and part fool's wisdom: if this is part of the rules, surely following the rules wards off bad luck.

The ten items guard against the contingencies of travel in mountains and woods: bad weather, getting lost, fatigue, a turned ankle. These things can happen so quickly on a hike or backpack trip that pessimism soon becomes second nature. Carrying the ten is simply insurance. The Indians walked light and fast, but they had a communal knowledge of nature's tools and foodstuffs which modern man has disowned.

1. **A compass.** (Preferably, a hiker learns how to use it beforehand. Outdoorsmen never get lost—but the scenery gets moved around.)

2. **Map.** Maps are for reading in the car, reading in the rain, checking against trail signs (vandals have a disconcerting habit of turning these to point in the wrong direction) and for reading on the summit of a mountain, to identify faraway peaks. Contour maps prevent unwelcome surprises. A cross-country ramble looks inviting and easy, but a moment's study of a map may show why hikers don't normally travel that way: a sheer rock cliff intervenes on the other side of that beguiling hill. A good map is like a friend along on the trip, silent and unobtrusive, but always ready with welcome suggestions.

3. **Knife.** Knives have many unexpected uses as well as the familiar. Cutting cheese for lunch. Whittling out a rainstorm. Cutting a piece of moleskin to comfort a blister. In fire-building and in first aid. Rock climbers even use knives to scrape out a convenient niche for a piton. Least expensive, and handy, is the traditional Boy Scout knife, which lends an air of frolic and youthful sport to many a sedate, middle-aged expedition. It usually combines folding blades, can opener, combination screwdriver and bottle opener—a modest but versatile instrument.

4. **Sunglasses.** Obviously essential on beaches and glaciers, where the powerful glare of sunrays hitting white sand or snow can cripple eyes; snowblindness is excessively painful.

5. **Matches.** Preferably carried in waterproof plastic case.

6. **Some kind of firestarter.** The campfire is no longer an acceptable custom, being wasteful of scarce timber, but in emergencies fires can save lives.

7. **First aid kit.** Drugstore prepackaged kits are usually inordinately expensive in their fancy wrappings. Far simpler, and less costly, to assemble a kit.

8. **Flashlight.** Trails descended in the dark are populated with surprise misfortunes and dangers: rocks, windfalls, vague turnings. Hikers hurrying downhill in fading light or darkness have missed corners and fallen off cliffs.

9. **Extra food.** Just in case. Items that hold up well are beef jerky, nuts, dried fruit. Food is quick energy for tired travelers, and a safeguard if the worst happens, getting hurt or lost with the resultant emergency bivouac.

10. **Extra clothing.** Again, just in case. The trail is simple: a short ramble to a viewpoint and the day is bright and sunny, but the weather has a mind of its own, which it often changes. Hikers who have ventured up easy mountain trails on the most gladsome of summer days have encountered sudden storms, apparently out of nowhere, and have come

away with frostbite or pneumonia or even hypothermia; they are lucky if they escape with their lives.

All the essentials fit handily in a modest rucksack. They take up little space and should never be removed.

A good many hikers romp in the mountains all year sans rope or even decent boots, encumbered by little more than fond visions of conquest or idealized memories of John Muir. Most hikers will be visited by mosquitoes, chapped lips, a few bruises, and various intimations of mortality. Such minor mountain maladies are nicely remedied by the ten essentials.

July 31

A July garden is populated with insects: aphids, damselflies, beetles.

Insects are considered to represent the lowest or purest form of instinct, yet sometimes display ingenuity; they are the most resourceful and prolific of nature's inventions. Nearly one million insect species have been counted on earth and a complete tally might total ten million, adapting to stagnant water, crude oil, sand, hot springs, freezing mountain streams, even red pepper. Insects look like salesmen's samples— tiny advertisements for a thousand colors and trademarks and costumes. Moths take on the color and shape of trees and leaves. Survival is often a game of let's pretend, as a harmless insect bluffs it out with frightening inflated face.

Tiny architects, insects construct elaborate galleries between the sapwood and bark of a tree, or construct huge cities of tunnels and mounds. Insects apparently live without mind, crude early steps on the evolutionary ladder of the nervous system, but some use tools: the wasp *Ammophila* tamps earth at the burrow entrance with a pebble held between the jaws. Insects exhibit both strength and immense powers of survival—a flea can jump 200 times the length of its body; insects have survived being frozen solid.

The range of sizes, colors and forms in the insect world is fantastic; more incredible is the entire alien complex machinery of the insect world, so different from man's vulnerable, bulky system, top-heavy with anxiety. The most riotous energies and experiments of nature abound in these tiny, multitudinously engineered bodies. In their dazzling range of colors, puzzling external skeletons, odd baffling eyes (the thousands of winking facets that make up the fly's mosaic eye), jewel and flower bodies, or bodies armored like tanks, insects seem the most spectacular and unrestrained of experiments. Insects will try anything several times.

August 1

Flowers are restful to look at. They are neither emotions nor conflicts.
—Sigmund Freud

August 2

Saint Francis of Assisi called him Brother Sun. On a warm glowing day the sun seems close and real, a neighbor we cannot look at directly but know to be a part of ourselves. In all life there is that response, that link; life flourishes under the sun because in each life there is that corresponding energy, the waiting flame. It takes the sun to warm the world, the Brother to wake his people.

August 3

A time for climbing mountains, now that the days are long, the wind gentle, the sun warm on the back, and dawn comes when night has barely begun, warming the peaks to life.

Years ago, gods lived in the high mountains, the angry Indian gods of the old volcanoes, the brooding demons that occupied the tormented uplifts of the Rockies.

Sir Leslie Stephen, the British mountaineer and early and audacious Victorian who made the mountains of Europe his playground, wrote that if he were to invent a new idolatry he would prostrate himself, not in any temple, but before one of those shadowy masses in which—despite all reason—it was impossible not to sense a brooding presence.

He was not altogether engaged in anthropomorphization. Stephen, like many other mountaineers, was a highly intelligent man who realized that mountains are the most visible, largest expressions of the earth's aliveness, in their jumbled upheavals and banked fires, and continue to change, though (usually) the changes are slow and subtle.

The earliest mountaineers did not climb to the summits at all, but were chamois hunters, or miners, or fur trappers. Not "because it is there"—not all men felt that challenge; the "what is there" was in man, and he populated the peaks with dragons.

To some degree, climbers conquer, or at least push to the limits a test of what is there, and in climbing, an electrical tension leaps to close the circuit. Every climber meets, on a mountain, something that is in opposition to himself, and yet part of himself, not too far away, in a sense, from what Paul Tillich called the ground of being.

On a slope, or a stern and uncompromising cliff, the body advances, while the mind seemingly does nothing, free of the clutter and anxiety of city life; here a climber is essentially alone, even if tied on the rope as part of a team, and a leap of faith takes him forward.

Old mountaineers dream of summits, of the gambols on the shattered cliff. In the most barren and sterile of mountains exists an essential reality. Mountains are structures of rocks and snow and ice, but cannot properly be dissected and classified any more than can dragons or gods.

August 4

Patterns of August: Seeds as flowers ripen and drop; heat haze a trembling web-veil; shimmer of beach sand. The world has a dense inchoate warmth, as if under glass.

August 5

THE SEED IS ALL

The month is one of ripening and fruition. Nature has one aim: the seed. Toward the production of the seed has gone nature's greatest efforts: the bud, the leaf, the blossom, the showy flower; programed into this sequence is the end result, the seed that will start the cycle all over again.

To get the seed from here to there, a variety of methods: seeds fly on the wind (the goatsbeard rides its own parachute), seeds ride piggyback on animals (sticky seeds of mistletoe, or barbed burdock and cocklebur, cling to furred mammals), seeds of one weed travel under their own umbrellas like friendly witches, jewelweed and touch-me-not eject seeds like bullets, and birds carry seeds undisturbed through their digestive tracts, often to surprising distances. One species of pine tree bears seeds that are released—in wind or on being touched—like the jet spray of an aerosol container.

Again and again the long extravagant process of growth and death, so that the restless seeds in their great numbers will crowd the earth—and a few will take hold and grow once more.

August 6

The mourning dove is gathering the seeds of harvest. To many, the gentle sound of the small, slender bird, so much like a replica of its extinct cousin, the passenger pigeon, is a plaintive drawn-out cooing—a sound of grief for the birds that once darkened the sky and now are gone. To others, the limpid sound is reassurance, and they have thought they heard in its harp-strum, "Never fear! I am here!"

Much like a domestic pigeon, the mourning dove is a ground feeder, walking about to glean seeds of weeds and grasses, searching in little flocks the fields in autumn for grains, then scurrying about on country roads to find needed bits of gravel and tiny stones for digestive aids. A few berries and worms will be eaten. Nest building is a casual affair: sometimes simply two eggs are laid in a depression on the ground; at other times the bird erects a thin nest in a tree.

A mild-colored bird of beige-brown, the dove is brightly spotted with pink and blue, and when it flies, its long pointed tail reveals white outer feathers. Although a game bird (despite demands for its protection), the dove is probably not in danger of immediate extinction, but will continue its gentle and melancholy call. These are the folk songs of nature.

August 7

On a hot August afternoon, rattlesnakes lie coiled like old men half-asleep, under rocks, under old rotting porches, at the mouths of caves. Sluggish and groggy snakes have been known to lie stretched across a shady section of trail where hikers have (gingerly) stepped around the listless object. Yet a rattler can strike faster than a camera's click; close up, its raised flattened viper head is the personification of hostility and malice toward all. Rattlesnakes are found throughout the United States in a great variety of species, in heavy concentrations in the Southwest and the South, difficult to eradicate and undeniably dangerous (a person bitten by a Mohave Green, depending on various factors, is said to have a life expectancy of perhaps seven minutes); yet relatively few Americans die each year of rattlesnake bites.

A small number suffer the consequences of bites in permanently damaged legs or ankles. Calm, restricted motion and swiftness of access to medical treatment are the keys to recovery; experienced hikers carry simple snakebite kits which are as much amulets perhaps as remedies, and psychological reminders to watch before putting hands trustingly on rock ledges. The venom, expelled through lethally efficient fangs, is a protein substance, its virulence depending on the age of the snake, its last meal, and perhaps the season. The rattlesnake appears a remarkable example of overkill; venom that would kill a 185-pound man is embodied in a hunter of jackrabbits.

The snake's reaction—fast and often without any warning—seems the perfect act of blind irrational brutality; actually the rattler prefers nothing more than being left alone (a captured snake may refuse to eat and buys freedom at the cost of his life) and is quick to defend any sensed intrusion of that dim and somnolent domain which is his. At dusk, he is awake, attentive to the business of living, creeping in search of rodents. A rattlesnake atop rocks in the darkness may rattle his alarm to an approaching camper. The rattle appears to be an evolutionary mechanism, and is not a warning so much as an instinctive nervous gesture. To anyone who has once heard it, the rattle is an unmistakable sound; it has been compared to a buzzing teakettle, to the hiss of steam, and sounds in truth much like the crackle of a high-tension wire.

Impressive in size and possessing a kind of primitive, prehistoric courage, the rattlesnake does hear airborne sounds, possesses a keenly sensitive tongue, and a well-protected brain. He is sinuously beautiful—patterned in his flowing diamond- or wedge-shaped, gleaming scales.

Professional snake hunters soon become routinely casual and nonchalant in handling their pronged sticks and nets, but never forget the potential of the creature they deal with. Cowboys and pioneers respected the rattlesnake, even while they tried to drive him from their lands. To many, the rattlesnake, harshly efficient, and as glaringly, oddly fascinating as the desert which is his frequent habitat, is a symbol still of the crude brute spirit of the frontier: "Don't tread on me!"

August 8

Follow a mountain stream uphill, and pass through the succession of life zones in subtle sequence, nourished and supported by the stream. John Burroughs called such a stream a "liquid harp." Indians and early settlers heard in the flowing waters living "river voices"; at night, a solitary camper may hear in the spill of water almost human voices that seem at times to call, or chant, or to instruct. It is the living tongue of the mountain, and an abundance of life and growth follows its course, even as the stream takes away, and restores.

Beginning as a spring or flow from an ice-bound lake, fed by snowmelt, the stream is at its liveliest and most aggressive in the spring, released from winter silence; by late summer, it is a diminished but still exuberant thing—a handspan leap takes the hiker across what was once a crescendo torrent. Even in August, a high mountain stream obeys the cycles of day and night, becoming quieter under cooler temperatures and as the high snows harden.

All things know the stream: the bobbing water ouzel, the deer, the coyote, which forge their trails to its necessary waters, short-lived meadow flowers; in the lower woods, ferns and mosses grow lush along its banks. Every half-mile of the long descent downhill is marked by change: from the stern requirements of the near arctic conditions of the alpine snowfields and rills, to the coursing canyons and pools of the forest river. Moss and algae grow in the slowed currents of pools, in tiny microhabitats; caddisflies and mayflies cling to stones, and trout and salmon spawn on the sandy bottom.

In August, the transparent, speaking stream is for watching slippery reflections, learning to know leaf patterns, for the patient study of stones.

August 9

The Sisters wilderness in central Oregon combines some of the most tenderly beautiful mountain scenery anywhere with some of the most grotesque. Scarred volcanic pinnacles alternate with the shining glass cliffs of black obsidian; the frail meadows of Husband Lake bloom—for a little while—in the shadow of ragged peaks like crude slagpiles. North Sister was climbed late; it is an inhospitable mix of steep-tilted ice and devilishly loose rock, and a relatively secure chimney that often freezes to a disconcerting slipperiness. Today the area is thronged with Boy Scouts, fishermen, climbers, and people hoping for a glimpse of the shy Sasquatch, but the ice slope of North Sister can still induce a respectful attention to steps and a subdued silence.

On August 9, 1910 H. H. Prouty finally conquered the "black beast" he had failed on twice before, and wrote his achievement on a handkerchief. In those days, many of the pioneers climbed as if they had already thrown their hats over the peaks. It was a point of pride, not only to be the first, but often to travel alone, lightly encumbered, to prove—somehow—that man was as much as, or more than a mountain. It was a time of curious innocence; few climbers used rope and most had scarcely heard of pitons, and the zest of the thing was in the very novelty of the undertaking: who knew what lay on the other side?

August 11

The dog days end. The weather is still hot—an August forenoon can be a heavy, pressing, breathless interlude; the thermometer climbs. Three o'clock in the afternoon is usually the hottest time of the day, and heat lingers, stifling and close, even after the sun goes down. The earth seems to hang fixed at the high turn of the wheel in the sun's eye. But August mornings foretell the change; each morning there is a cooler mistiness, an almost imperceptible graying and dampening of the sky. The air has the smell of September in it. With slowness and deliberation, the earth is cooling as the hours of light grow shorter.

August 12

STAR TRACKING

On a bland August night the stars are brilliant and close; the sky is all stars, like a thousand lighted rooms.

Diving stars slide across the sky—the swift brilliant flight of the Perseid meteor shower. Now, the earth, as in every year, enters clouds of fragments rushing through space, streaming from the constellation of Perseus. As these stars reach the earth's atmosphere, friction turns them incandescent and they flame briefly across the sky. Each meteor, passing at a speed of twenty miles a second, flames into brilliance when it is at perhaps a height of sixty miles. It rushes on into the void, vanishes. The quick thin leap of flame repeats as another star flashes by on its unimaginable journey. After midnight the most spectacular displays will occur, when the earth, rotating in the opposite direction of the stream of meteors, meets face to face the blaze and brilliance of these errant stars. Other stars, unmoving, pulse; flashing green-white, darkening, they seem to flicker and almost disappear, then blaze again.

On such a night, it is possible to sense—however faintly—the rightness of the whole, the calm and unhurried travels of the universe. Stars like flowers are innocent and serene in the sky, for man's enjoyment. On the other hand, the universe may be contemplating man.

August 13

A few years ago, an old man lived on Mount Shasta, in a crude arrangement of tent fastened between the pines on the lower slope of the mountain, well away from the normal climbing and hiking routes. He was obviously a mildly deranged but harmless individual, people thought, a hermit in his retreat, an individual without family or funds, finding a temporary existence here in the summer.

People who live around the mountain or climb it often have become accustomed to its collection of amusing eccentrics and tolerant of fanatics; Shasta is said to harbor a long-vanished race of strange third-eye people, of great but vague and inexplicable wisdoms, and some of the spiritist and psychic cults for which California is famous flourish at the base of the mountain. No one worried much or paid much attention to the old man, who seemed agreeable enough—for a hermit—stopping occasionally in his solitary travels to chat with a hiker or a climber. He had somewhat the air of a displaced prophet, with his ragged faded clothes and a great, flourishing beard. He had—it is true—a few odd habits; he always carried a shovel on his travels here and there around the mountain, which he said gave him balance in crossing the glacier and the ice. Shasta, for all its serenity, and its appeal to poets ("white and lonely as the moon"), has its threat of loose rock and frozen slopes. The body of a dead dog was found on the climbing route. People have hiked here with pets, and in school parties; a few have come to grief.

Too, the old man had a disconcerting habit of appearing suddenly, unexpectedly and seemingly out of nowhere; never on the summit, though, no higher than the first stiff-frozen snow penitentes of Lake Helene, near the mountaintop. The summit, the old man said, he would reserve for later; he had not yet visited there. He continued on his solitary wanderings—looking for gold? a vision? or perhaps simply for food?—and two skiers reported they saw him in the winter. Weeks would pass, and then he would be back again, surfacing now and then like a creature of the past, a Loch Ness monster.

One summer the climbers returned, the customary mountaineers of the Sierra Club and the Mazamas, and it was not until much later—late in August toward the end of the climbing season—that someone remarked that no one at all had seen the old man that summer.

August 14

Captain E. D. Pearce led a small party up Mount Shasta August 14, 1854, and raised the flag on the summit at twelve noon. So much for a dignified ascent in proper military fashion; the men slid and coasted downhill, outrageously racing each other, and finally crashed and rolled to a stop at the foot of the mountain. They picked themselves up and assessed injuries, still blithe spirits: "We found that some were minus hats, some boots, some pants, and others had their shins bruised. . . ."

August 15

Some people go camping, one suspects, not so much for the fun of it, as to teach nature (and only incidentally themselves) a lesson. There are those outfitted in trailer rigs so top-heavy with motorbikes and boats that a truck driver would hesitate to drive them. Others arrive at chosen spots with full facilities, having written well ahead for reservations, bringing their own radios, lights, and refrigerators, unwilling to release the cords of civilization. Others, getting early into an uncrowded campground, nervously head for a spot next to the only other camper. These are people like children newly in school, having much to learn. Some of them can never be taught. At the other extreme is the backpacker who practices a martyrdom of traveling light, often to the point of risk. The ultimate in modern-day camping is the commuter camper: mother and youngster stay in the tent while the father goes off to work every day, driving as much as sixty miles each way and coping with slightly wrinkled clothes and a schizophrenic attitude of making the best of two worlds.

In actuality, the essence of camping is not a matter of tents and gear and building fires; the spirit of camping has little to do with equipment, but is a simplicity, a restoration. For true campers: darkness, silence—minus lanterns, or radios, or even other people. Camping is, of course, a suspension of time, an acceptance of impermanence and insecurity, and campers develop or possess—possibly it is bred in the genes—a willingness to become, at least partly and for a while, part of the night and the woods and the silent realm. In general, women, the nest builders, are less fond of camping, preferring more comfortable and stable environments, which would argue that a taste for the elemental, which is the highest sophistication, may not be instinct, but conditioning, or cultivated taste. Louise Bogan, the poet, wrote: "Women have no wilderness in them, they are provident instead."

As population increases and the lands of national forests and parks shrink, camping may become a thing of the past, an odd amusement, an anachronistic pastime for dilettantes.

August 16

Late afternoon. In the brilliant musky heat, a sudden thunderstorm like a seizure that rocks the sky.

A yellow tension precedes the storm; dogs become restless and the immediate area may be silent of birds. The air seems heavy and full of an almost audible silence. Lightning occurs when the currents and clouds play leapfrog, simulating a particularly lethal Russian roulette. Air, rising higher, gathers and freezes. Positive electric charges form at the top of the thunderhead, negative below, in tense attraction to the positive charges on the ground. The opposition of these charges forms and opens a thin iodized channel up the air, down which the slim hot snake of lightning leaps. The stab sears trees, burns holes, cracks rock. Selective and erratic at the same time, lightning does strike twice in the same place, can destroy a patriarch tree while the occupants of a house watch a few feet away, can kill a human or simply maim him for life. In the mountains, a lightning display leaps across an entire basin; a ricocheting crash and tympani of thunder echoes from rock cliff to cliff.

The old saying, "If you can hear the thunder you're safe," is less than reassuring when an ear-splitting clap is followed immediately by a stab of light that fills an entire sky.

The storm passes quickly—earliest people believed these brassy shows to be the temper displays of angered gods—and rain falls, heavy fast rains that, too, are soon over, and leave the cooling ground smelling fresh and sweet.

At night, after a long hot day, sultry and oppressive with heavy-hanging heat, there is often a brilliant erratic display of heat lightning, tongue flickers along the horizon, almost always silent and remote, then moving on without a sound.

August 17

A sound like a doorknocker in the forests and orchards: the steady rapping of the friendly and engaging downy woodpecker.

The little lumberjack is at work again. Persons chopping wood have on occasion been startled to find that the sounds of their activity have fetched curious downy woodpeckers or the larger pileated woodpecker.

The bird leaves behind evidence of his work in riddled wood, but he has hunted out and eaten the insects most injurious to trees: gall insects, maple and birch borers, pine weevils, coddling moths, and apple borers. For his work, a well-equipped skull and bill; the brain is protected by its structure against the blows of the heavy repeated drumming. Softer-voiced than its larger relatives, the downy male, with his bright scarlet cap, does not sing at all in mating, but vigorously displays his prowess in a round of athletic drumming.

Trustful of man, the downy woodpecker can be lured to country dooryards with bits of food. Birds that have become accustomed to being thus fed will sometimes rap imperiously on the door—a serious and businesslike signal.

August 18

On August 18, 1870, General Hazard Stevens and Philomen Beecher Van Trump reached the summit of Mount Rainier—the great white Takhoma.

The mountain had been tried many times; most notable was the attempt of Lieutenant Katz, who made a strenuous eighty-mile approach from Fort Steilacoom, bringing rope, a hatchet, a thermometer, and "plenty of hard biscuit"—but failed to get higher than the upper snow dome.

Stevens and Van Trump had as guide a pessimistic Indian, Sluiskin, who led them on a roundabout and taxing route, climbing over the brushy Tatoosh range before bringing them to the beginning slopes of Rainier. A third companion, Edmund Coleman, who had climbed in the Alps and was weighted down with a variety of equipment, soon gave up the climb. For Stevens and Van Trump, further trials: as dusk settled and the campfire flickered and the tall mountain stood white and ghostly, Sluiskin began a long and melancholy dirge, warning the pair of grave perils, and hostile Indian gods. He sang all night; his audience slept fitfully. Equipped with rudimentary ice creepers, the two climbers did reach the summit, but so late in the day that they were forced to spend all night in the summit crater, alternately scalded on one side and freezing on the other. On the way down, they slipped and bounced and slid, and arrived, cut and bruised, to find an astonished Sluiskin, who approached them tentatively and in grave astonishment, hardly believing that they were still alive.

Stevens and Van Trump ate a rather dismal meal of roast marmot and rested; Sluiskin sang a different chant: "Skookum tillicum! Skookum tumtum!" (Strong men, brave hearts!)

August 19

The Cumberland River, flowing through Tennessee, beginning and ending in Kentucky, is still as green in places as in the time of its youth. It remains a river of deep woods, secretive hills, Indian legends, and lush moist vegetation, despite the dams built in the 1930s and the ambitious city of Nashville.

Along the Cumberland were proud and cruel battles between the Cherokee Indians, and the Iroquois and other tribes, and the whites. A vital artery of westward expansion, the Cumberland was traveled by flatboat and keelboat. Andrew Jackson and Daniel Boone knew the Cumberland; in those days the river was a clear green thing running wild and free through woods, and the rock cliffs and canebrake and tangled trees sheltered deer and bear in abundance.

In remote mountain country, men still plow tilted fields, and women work at archaic crafts, a group of people so remote and isolated from the rest of the country, estranged in a somber pocket of history, that they seem to lie hiding here, waiting for another rebirth, and the ugly stains of mining have polluted the streams that flow into the Cumberland.

The Cumberland is an old river, and its first people, the mysterious mound builders, are vanished. Survival is tenuous and the end may be predictable now for both the river and its inhabitants; there is no mystery in decay.

August 20

Summer is brief and ephemeral in the mountains; even in August it can rain—and rain. In any part of the country campers can be outwitted by rainstorms, and a cold cheerless fog blots out the trees and mountain shapes and the glowing pools of lakes that were so appealing a few days ago. At high elevations, quick but intense snowstorms whiten trails and rocks. Some campers bring cards and paperbacks to pass the time of waiting; others stand around grumbling and keep a cheerless tally: so many days lost.

In persistent fog and rain, when morning after morning is a chill awakening to mist and drizzle, and the slap of wet heather if one ventures reluctantly outside the tent, the camper is required to adopt a calm and Buddhalike indifference. Passive and unalarmed, wait out the rain, while drifting mists, moody as thoughts, invite meditation. Drink cup after cup of tea, become (temporarily) a Zen novitiate, half sleeping, half waking, half submerged and afloat in a trance-held world. Fog spills over the pass and the dim shapes of trees and cliffs appear and disappear; the mountain world flickers like a vision in the flame of a candle.

August 21

A glacier is a living thing. The glacier moves, shapes the mountain, breaks and divides its path down the mountainside, becomes a spilling river. Built of snow and ice, the glacier may be a thin streak of living white, or treacherous black ice looking like an innocent, dirty path, or the broad palatial highway of a gentled slope. Its life is in its movement, perceptible to measurements, and its visible power, crushing boulders, changing rock to the dust of the terminal moraine. Glaciers creep like spiders over old volcanoes like Mount Saint Helens, which is a comparatively young mountain and has little vegetation in the pumice slopes but gives indications of an alarming aliveness, and may erupt again. Mount Rainier has the largest number of glaciers—twenty-six— and the largest is Emmons, a broad, smooth and slippery highway, which has claimed the lives of climbers unlucky enough to lose their footing. Later in the summer, the glacier shows its age, pockmarked with stones and dust, wrinkled and seamed as crevasses open, gleaming a beautiful and perilous ice-blue in their secretive depths; a good-sized crevasse could easily swallow up an entire seven-story building. Toward the top of the mountain, the bergschrund is the giant crack where the living, advancing glacier first pulls away from the mountainside. Yosemite, where John Muir was the first to prove that the great domes and pinnacles were carved out by glacier action, from a distance suggests the look of glaciers still alive, in the sheen of light on the rough granite.

Glacier lassitude is a common phenomenon known to climbers, who, descending a mountain late on a hot August afternoon, snow-goggled and blindly following vague tracks, apathetic with heat and fatigue, stumble off the route and find themselves marching toward the edges of cliffs. A glacier, veined and seamed with crevasses, weighted with old snow, carries and crushes down the rocky soil; John Muir said, "The life of a glacier is one long grind."

August 22

The forest fire that starts in late summer—by a lightning stroke or a careless camper's match—is an ugly and "unnatural" disaster. The blackened, empty acres of great devastation of areas like the Tillamook Burn in Oregon stand as witness. Entire forests can be destroyed and its residents sacrificed; skeletons of trees attest the visit of the destroyer.

Yet a forest fire can be beneficial, and Smoky the Bear may have been wrong, or at least not altogether right; Forest Service officials have learned that fire may be helpful in some aspects, clearing the forest floor to make way for new plant growth, altering and renewing the mineral distribution of the soil. In chaparral areas, particularly, many seeds need the stimulus of fire to germinate, and now forestry management speaks of controlled burning, much as controlled hunting.

Controlled burning may even act to save an endangered species, like Kirtland's warbler, a rare songbird that must nest only in young jack pines of short height, and flourishes when seedlings spring up in burned-over land. Aspens grow where flames spread, and skies were dusk-reddened as bruises for days; in time evergreen seedlings will rise, and the aspens will be crowded out and die.

The catastrophe that destroys is also the agent of change and life.

August 23

America was in the beginning a land of harvest. The great plains—the heartland—was the cornucopia, and the pioneers moved slowly westward in the hope of finding the land of plenty. America was originally a nation of farmers; from the soil came dreams and each man's firm vision of independence. Iowa, Kansas, Nebraska—these were the country's granaries and pride. Before the cities, there was wheat.

Across the country now, the great stands of wheat still nod and sway, golden rippling dunes of the rolling wheatlands, in the Dakotas, Oklahoma, in eastern Washington in Snake River country. Wheat is still the staff of life.

In the Midwest, a man's hopes can rise and fall with the year's crop; wheat is gold currency. Farmers still trust to chance and the weather; a sudden thunder and hail storm can mean the loss of thousands of dollars if a field is trampled down, or parched in a drought.

Machinery and irrigation take some of the risk out of wheat farming; in the dry powdery plains of the Snake River the land is made arable. Experimental plots yield over 200 bushels an acre, under modern technology and airplanes that spray, fertilize, and give the growing wheat an extra boost of water.

For most farmers, though, the dream of independence is a thin one, and the stubborn pride rooted in the soil a chancy gamble on the past. The price tag on the dream is high. Irrigation is expensive: a self-propelled, center-pivoted sprinkler that can cover a circular field of 140 acres 20 times in 24 hours will cost over $25,000. Without irrigation, much of the land turns chalk-dry in August, powdery "alkali" that drifts like smoke under tractor wheels. In the plains states, a tornado can spectacularly harvest the gold grain in a brutal funnel of destruction.

With luck, the farmer can make a living, and barter his gold currency, but not for wealth, and modern processing methods strip the wheat of its vigor; the pallid and spongy loaf at the grocer's little resembles the bread that held yesterday's body and soul together.

But on an August noon, under the idle gaze of the sun, the land looks as it must have looked years ago—tall and swelling gold, sunflower-bordered, the land of promise.

August 24

In high mountain country, campers move with discretion. The halcyon, innocent days of the group outings are no more, when forty-sixty members of a mountain club went into the lakes and meadows and set up a great, jovial camp, complete with latrines and mess tents and proceeded in all innocence to demolish the mountain setting. In some wilderness areas, Enchantment Lakes, for example, even campfires are not now allowed (why burn the scarce, silvery wood that is one of the picturesque reasons for coming here?). The approach now realizes that even the most well-meaning mountaineer has an impact upon the land, and the land of wilderness is fragile and vulnerable. In other popular areas, the popularity of a favorite setting has been its ruin. At Mowich Lake in Mount Rainier National Park the delicate heather and meadow flowers and grasses were trampled and stripped bare by visitors who loved too much and unwisely in their enthusiasm. No meadow camping at all is allowed now; the Park Service has spread the devastated area with bags of Beautibark in an effort to rebuild the soil, and the only camping is allowed in the paved parking area—aluminum bullet trailers and elegant Winnebagos crowd in a grotesque circle, faithful to the ideal if not the fact.

The rule has long been: take only pictures, leave only footprints. Now, campers try to walk delicately, and leave not even the record of their steps. In part, modern quality equipment makes conservation-conscious camping possible.

Freeze-dried foods leave little weight to be packed out in plastic bags. A fast dependable cartridge stove is lightweight, and if less romantic than a campfire, leaves no scars on the ground. Bough beds are unthinkable; down sleeping bags are light in weight and warm at lowest temperatures. Only in a near-emergency is ditching around a tent justifiable, and on departure, the ground is restored. No garbage is buried; bears are keen-scented diggers.

All conservation is essentially a habit, an attitude; the aim is to go away leaving a campsite looking as if it had never been visited. The delicacy and fragility of the high meadows are their attraction: the flower-decked, pathless scene, the granite boulders that mark secret tarns, tree branches like lace in fog. In such a setting, the visitor moves gently and thoughtfully, trying to disturb as little as possible, and quickly learns habits of discipline and austerity. Even his voice is quieter, he absorbs the high silence, and a shout across a mountain lake seems a blasphemy.

August 26

The Chumash Indians of southern California had an ingenious method for hunting deer. The Indian, armed with bow and arrow, pulled over himself the hide of a slain deer, fixing it over his head so that only his eyes looked out. In this guise, perhaps for a little time feeling much like a deer himself, senses sharpened by the journey of risk, he crept in and out of bushes, crouched in the chaparral, went furtively among the trees to stalk his fellow animal. Hunting was, of course, part of the subsistence pattern; no Chumash hunted for the fun of it. The rituals and the purification of the temescal and the charmstones brought to the shaman helped ensure good luck—but also reminded the Chumash of the essential fact: this was another living thing that they were killing, in order to live themselves.

No Chumash Indian would have recognized the phrase "reverence for life," although the Chumash were skeptical (perhaps) of the Christian's smug insistence on that imaginary gulf between animals and divinely created man. A Chumash killed, it is known, when it was necessary, and the killing for survival took on a grace and a dignity, an act done in prayer and composure like a sacrament. All of the dead deer was used: the meat sustained life, the antlers were tools for flaking arrowpoints, the hide became clothing, and the sinew bound together that ingenious canoe, the tomol.

No anthropologist suggests that the Chumash killed in compassion; that is an attitude that arrives late after the event. Only highly civilized cultures with their record of variously motivated wars and murders can claim compassion for their mutual victims, but the Chumash went purified to the hunt, to the necessary act, and moved in silence, like the deer.

August 28

"The wilderness experience" is a term grandly and loosely used by the U.S. Forest Service, in glossy brochures which usually show a wholesome family group departing into the woods, gallantly ready to cope with such hazards as spiders, an occasional rainstorm, or rocky trails.

In actuality, most people have only the vaguest idea of what wilderness is, and have never seen it, let alone experienced it. To the majority, wilderness is defined by what it is not: no radio, no showers, no supermarket, no street lights. The San Jacinto wilderness is beautiful, and undeniably serene much of the time, but possesses fifty-four miles of trail, and is a half-hour away from the civilized delights of Palm Springs; it is in fact a large park, to a great degree man-made.

A young man writing recently in one of the outdoor magazines tells of trying to recreate the wilderness experience. He had a friend with a private plane take him to a remote mountain area in northern Canada. Here there were no roads, no trails, only a vaguely mapped area of mountains and lakes; after his friend had departed, not even the sound of planes. Man is a conditioned animal, and now there were almost none of the familiar stimuli, only the unmarked wild setting of a forgotten evolutionary past. Surely this—if anything could be—was the wilderness experience.

It was August, and the days were mellow, but the nights cool; there was evidence of large animals traveling near the lake shores. The silence, at first welcoming, soon became disquieting; the camper found himself listening, half hoping, for the familiar. Solitude imposes a responsibility of attentiveness.

After a couple of days, he realized he was not, in truth, experiencing wilderness—not at least as he had thought he could duplicate the conditions of true participation. He had light, modern down bag and parkas, freeze-dried foods; the knowledge that his friend would return in a few days. Even had he attempted to live on wild plants and possibly small animals, it would have seemed a curiously deliberate, artificial exercise in discomfort. He knew that a highway lay beyond a couple of ridges, and that he was essentially an observer in this lonely place, weighted down with all the habits and expectations of his normal narrow existence.

The wilderness experience is impossible to create, and this is the reason so many outdoor survival outings fail; it is a game rather than reality ("you may advance to the next camp"), and the superficial novelty of the situation imposes on the mind, rather than the underlying reality. Soon the young man found himself restless, nervously aware of his own predilection for comfort, uneasy with night sounds and anxious for new scenery. The experience had become curiously disappointing and flat; he felt ill at ease both with himself and the setting.

Even in a synthetic facsimile, the wilderness experience is probably unbearable to live with, like meeting God face to face.

August 29

In the hottest stretch of August, hikers have died on the Goat Rocks, or on the slopes of Mount Washington in the East.

Mountain weather can change suddenly, and chilling and fatigue produce the lethal combination of hypothermia:

The drop in temperatures, the sudden snow, act with the brief brutal intensity of a tropical storm. Hikers who think they can keep going ("it's only a little ways to shelter") stumble, become glassy-eyed, grope unsteadily toward imaginary companions. Hikers who have not carried extra clothing, or fail to put it on, rapidly lose body heat and yield to exhaustion, and, swiftly, release; death by freezing is a kind, painless end. The art of survival is to underestimate one's own strength, and never forget the calm enduring strength of the mountains.

August 31

In August:

Lie in a hammock (drink lemonade and read an immense novel)

Go berrying

Contemplate the sky and its clouds

Sit at the edge of a lake

Walk around a farm; observe the whisper of a breeze across a field, a moving cloud of gnats, in no hurry, the rightness and orderliness of a dog in its fur

Straddle a fence and chew on a blade of grass

The earth seems at its highest point, a tilting climax in its union with the sun, hanging calm and suspended before the long ride downhill.

September 1

Labor Day is the date of human migration. On this afternoon, throughout the country, long lines of fitfully stalled and impatiently creeping traffic: trailers, vans, campers, cars with tents or boats strapped to the top. The journey back has begun. Leaving behind the crowded campsites and parks and beaches, the human migrates to city and school and job.

If the day is hot, tempers will match, and there is always the rash of accidents; some migrating individuals will not complete the trip. On a narrow mountain road with no eye now for the scenery that was so alluring two or three weeks ago, a motorist yells at another: "Why don't you look where you're going?" "Listen, I'm in a hurry—" Youngsters, surfeited with cool lakes and rambles in the woods, groan at the thought of school starting again. Home sounds like a haven to their mothers, and the sunburned and insect-bitten yearn for a little quiet and private peace.

A few clouds overhead. The last two mornings have been frost-spangled; the woods quickly become chilly, inhospitable places, and a wind blows like a door slamming shut. A hiker rests at the trailhead; his pack is lighter after two weeks' walking, he is thinner, and his muscles harder. He senses both achievement and a frustration: "It gets more crowded every year."

Going home. Someone is boarding up the cabin by the lake, and in the little Last Chance store the owner counts the take from fishing tackle and maps and stomach remedies. A ranger inspects vandal damage to a restroom. In a few days the water will be turned off. Signs (Nature Program Tonight) are taken down. The campgrounds turn quiet as the last cars leave.

Did anyone remember to lock up the wilderness?

September 2

Patterns of September: Vein tracings of a leaf. Cloud trace across the sky. From burning leaves, smoke fingers trace purposeful directions. Departing birds track orderly patterns as precise as a map.

September 3

Nature abhors emptiness. After a forest fire, fireweed rushes in to fill the blackened empty spaces and cover up the devastation. A profuse and pretty job of patchwork: the plant is tall—two to six feet, lavish with pink/magenta and purple blossoms. At the very top of the stalk, above the lance-shaped green leaves and the shiny flowers, green miniature bells hang. Seeds are whiskery with white down.

Now in September, the flower is brilliant and handsome as it spreads in open woods and decorates the fire-blighted spots; later it will be untidy and disheveled as the seeds drop.

Fireweed may grow for years in shaded forest, lacking vigor; fire gives it its day in the sun. With the increased sunlight in newly opened space, fireweed is stimulated to spread rapidly and create many more seeds.

This is a pioneer plant, and like any pioneer, it is hardy, making few demands on soil or moisture. An opportunist, it seizes the chance to colonize where it can.

September 4

Atmosphere is the placental membrane of the world, and on a September day, cooling earth and cooling air give the sky a fresher clarity. At the same time, interruptions of fog and mist, or the mellowness of an occasional warm day that gives the air a transient density; September is a veiled haze. Nourished in a girdle of constantly changing, perpetually unchanging air, the ball of earth spins—crude clay and rock hung in space—and the light recedes.

September 6

Sphagnum moss is a delicate and gray-green festoon on the surface of moist bogs.

During the First World War, hikers collected the moss during the spring and summer and gathered in the fall to complete the makings of surgical dressings. The very soft moss, cleaned and dried, was a highly absorbent filter in the pads, which used also non-absorbent cotton, absorbent paper, and an outside covering of moss. Sphagnum has the desirable quality of being light and fluffy, and does not pack.

Organizations—the Mountaineers' Sphagnum Auxiliary was one—sat in clubrooms to fashion the dressings, often completing 700 or more a month to be sent to France and England.

Sphagnum moss grows abundantly around cranberry marshes, and in the forest and among hardhack in wet places. Favored places of abundant growth were visited in sociable romps; girls who had walked to collect the moss and now put together the dressings talked as they worked and made plans for happier trips—even as they made the bandages for unthinkable injuries—for when the boys returned from over there.

September 7

The woods are made for the hunters of dreams, the brooks for the fishers of song. . . . To the hunters who hunt for the gunless game the streams and the woods belong.

–Sam Walter Foss

September 8

Apples ripen, turn to golden yellow and red. Jonathan, Baldwin, Northern Spy, McIntosh. The names have a sociable, convivial sound. The apple is a sociable fruit, lending itself to family and social functions where it may turn up in pies or cobblers.

Cider is a fall drink, stout and pleasing. Not as many families make cider as once did, when the process was an annual one conducted with all the solemn merriment that attends a ceremonial function. The end product, if thoughtfully "neglected" a bit, becomes hard cider. The most respectable and strait-laced of early settlers, who considered themselves the most temperate of men, would drink hard cider (the harder the better) and never bat an eye. Cider is for drinking on fall nights, before a fire on a chilly evening that is blue-cool and crisp. As American as apple cider!

September 9

Pride of New England is the sugar maple, ablaze now in the fall and decorating entire countrysides with leaves shining yellow and orange through deep red. The romantic days of the sugarbush are gone; the panoply of kettles and open fires have yielded to Yankee technology, but the sugar maple is still a fine and useful thing, valued not only for its sweetness but its excellent durable wood and the handsome pattern of bird's-eye maple.

On a September afternoon in the East, long lines of cars move slowly and often stop; beauty creates a traffic jam.

September 10

Migrant birds depart; the monarch butterfly takes its leave.

After years of study, scientists still do not know exactly what triggers migration or by what process a departing bird chooses his route.

Choice of leave-taking time, pattern of departure—all these seem familiar and obvious and simple, yet ultimately without explanation; riders on a spinning wheel, the migrants move like the tides.

Not always do the departures seem hurried. Monarchs, brightly costumed, parade south, pausing to sip nectar. Swallows fly away, feeding as they go; their departure has a milling, jostling air of excitement. More disciplined, the herons and other shorebirds gather in orderly flocks to begin the exodus. Many kingbirds are already gone.

Autumn migrations over eastern mountains are spectacular; enthusiasts plan a year ahead to visit favorite high lookouts like Hawk Mountain in Pennsylvania. Here the onlooker gazes down on the rapt, intense flight of hundreds of birds in a day. A record flight occurred in September of 1948—11,392 hawks were counted.

For thousands of years, birds and butterflies have migrated, with urgency or without, leaving no letter of farewell. A built-in restlessness, perhaps, like migrant berry pickers and crop gatherers, who keep moving, uneasy with civilization. "Instinct" ultimately is a catch-all term, a meaningless phrase that covers sensory response to stimuli, early conditioning, reaction to parental and species behavior, an individual awareness of cooling temperature and the slowly contracting days.

September 11

Anthropologists call them "balanophagists"—those Indians for whom acorns were a principal part of the diet. Adaptable and resilient, Indians along the coast of central California turned inland in the autumn to gather seeds and berries and the ubiquitous acorn.

Preparing acorns involved several steps: women (food-gathering was woman's work and presumably children's) garnered the acorns and brought them to the large mortarholes hollowed out in the rocks of the hills. Archaeologists will not vouch for anything that cannot be directly proved by the evidence, but it is possible to reconstruct the scene: women in little groups of two or three, sitting on the warm sandstone boulders, chatting as they cracked open the acorns and dropped the meat into holes. Gnarled low-hanging oaks guarded the secretive streams; meager game trails were routes for Indian feet. Birds—considerably more then than now—circled and spun overhead in the bright firm sky. September could be tranquil, but there was work to be done, and quickly.

Now, with stone pestles, women ground the acorns into meal. The life of an Indian woman was literally a grind; from the days of childhood on she would be fashioning the great stone bowls, grinding out the smooth center and shaping the bowl, then grinding the acorns that were food between the times of fishing and the lucky hunt. Raw acorn meal has a bitter taste, the pungent acridity of tannic acid. Another scene: these women, kneeling by a fire, pouring boiling water again and again over the meal. After several washings, the leached meal, now light in color, was fit to eat. The meal would figure in the winter diet as a kind of porridge, or cakes cooked on a stone slab like a griddle.

The Indians were not agriculturists. They simply used what was available and moved between ocean and inland hills, environ-

mentalists in the sense of following nature's patterns rather than imposing patterns of their own.

Tannic acid is considered to be poisonous to some degree; it
is known that cattle will abort after eating it.

The gentle Indian women, brought to the early missions
often by force, and bewildered by the new rules and an alien way of life,
converted suddenly and sometimes brutally to the melancholy suffer-
and-repent philosophy of Christianity, bore no more living babies, and
soon died themselves. Some researchers believe the women ate raw
acorns to bring on miscarriages. In a few years, entire cultures were
wiped out; an estimated ten to twelve thousand Chumash Indians
vanished as if they had never lived.

In the yellow-brown chaparral-covered hills, the mortarholes are still in the rocks, mute evidence of quiet lives.

September 12

Jack Frost gets credit for work he never does. Artist frost may
decorate windowpanes and adorn trees and bushes with ice crystals, but
he is no painter of the changing trees.

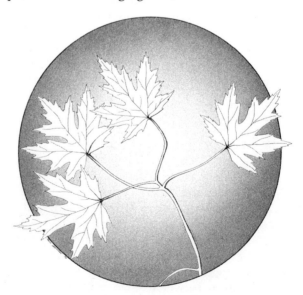

Now the leaves begin to turn yellow or flame red or burnt sienna, not so much because of frost and cooling temperatures, though these play a part (frost, striking too early, turns leaves a premature November brown, the dead-dry color of winter), but because the shortening days stop the production schedule of these ingenious factories.

The time-clock of a tree is geared to light. As daylight diminishes, circulation slows and chlorophyll dwindles. The strong yellow pigments remain: birch and aspen turn gold; in other trees (some maples and most oaks) other pigments, from sugars remaining in the leaves, turn the leaves crimson.

Production stops, the leaves are sealed off, and the elements of life and activity all go back into the trunk and root.

All summer a bounty of green leaves, as chlorophyll converted the air to food for the tree. Leaves, their work done, are tossed aside by-products, now expendable and excess, to be discarded as the drying leaf, sealed off from the tree, withers and drops.

Waste-products, in a sense, and an intimation of mortality; yet the leaves in their last stages are perhaps most beautiful—a bold and gaudy assertion of sunset color. At the very end of their usefulness, leaves become their most vivid, noticeable, and individual.

September 13

A hiker hurrying along Hurricane Deck in the California wilderness sensed that he was being rudely followed. He had heard stories of people following the narrow trail here; just below the steep rim of the ridge, along shattered rocks and thorny tangles of brush, abandoning caution and running because of swooping wails close at their heels, then hearing the careening unseen screamer rush past. Now, every time he glanced back, he saw only yellow and gray-brown yucca and manzanita along the unshaded bowls of hills and ravines—no secrets here, no place for anything to hide. Then he saw a mountain lion, cat-supple, move between the rocks.

A party driving across the plains of eastern Oregon at eight in the morning looked idly out the car windows at empty fields. An immense cat like a statue sat guarding a burrow. The mountain lion simply watched them as they stopped the car and excitedly leaped out. It waited until they had clambered across the ditch and into the field before it moved slowly and easily away, drifting out of their sight.

A forest ranger woke one night in his unbuttoned tent, after he dreamed that his face was being licked by a rough tongue, and found himself staring into a mountain lion's gravely solicitous eyes.

Shy of man, elusive as a sun mote in a dark forest, the mountain lion is still that much of a cat—at times showing a persistent feline curiosity.

The animal—variously called puma, painter, catamount, cougar—is the very color of an autumn leaf. Perfectly at ease in his habitat of rocks and trees, he is an agile climber and solitary, skillful hunter.

People shudder at the supposed ferocity of the lion, who, hardly kitten-tame, has never made a recorded attack on an adult man. There have been maulings of children—probably because the puma was teased, or a child may have presented an attractive, small target when normal prey was scarce.

Pumas have also aroused the anger of farmers and stockmen, who indiscriminately kill the big cats, explaining the slaughter on the basis of lost sheep and cattle. In actuality, the puma is a useful predator, keeping deer populations in check.

Fewer in number now, the mountain devil of early days lingers on, more shy and secretive than ever. He is big; a puma may be seven and a half feet long and weigh 175 pounds or more. His voice is no less impressive, a raspy cough or growl, and persons claim to have heard a high ripsaw scream that is the very sound of wilderness. The puma likes plenty of cover; the mother bears her young on well-hidden rock ledges. Playful kittens, the cubs early learn to adopt the motions and manners of the hunt. The face of the puma is big and tom-solid, whiskered with extremely sensitive antennae. Yellow eyes look out impassively at a hostile world.

A puma shot by a cattle rancher is (perhaps) a cow or two saved, but one less American lion, one more voice silenced. The wilderness will be an empty thing when all the voices are gone.

September 14

This month, the bells of nature ring for those who will listen: the big-bell voices of big-leaved trees as wind tosses the maples, the mellow lower-pitched sound of wind humming in the pines and firs, now and again a pulsing vibration. The ragged hoot of an owl. Birds are choristers, singing out the last song before departure. Crickets chime in accord to the softer bells. Leaf sounds, as in the quietness the leaves fall. The bells of nature ring.

September 16

The woodchuck—February's groundhog—is an early-to-bed sort. Now, fat and bleary-eyed with clover and vegetables, he prepares for hibernation.

Increasingly lethargic, he sits at the burrow entrance, motionless, awaiting some final signal to begin his long sleep. Chubby, but still reasonably attentive, for woodchuck are preyed on by the red fox and by man.

As a weather prophet he is much overrated, and has some unlikeable abilities: he piles mounds of earth at the burrow door that can wreck tractors. New Hampshire, in 1883, heartily disliking the woodchuck, placed little value on him: a ten-cent bounty. A small animal, four to ten pounds, he manages to eat a pound of green food a day.

Drowsy and replete, he will enter his home by one of several doors. There, underground tunnels branch and twist up to forty feet. The groundhog makes a bed of grass, yields to sleep, and may—or may not—emerge again February 2.

September 17

Quaking aspens are a gold shimmer in the fall, making up in a burst of evanescent prettiness for a previously undistinguished life. The tree was considered worthless by early loggers because the wood is soft, and the tree has a queasy susceptibility to fungus diseases and heart rot; many trees die before the age of fifty, like a race of weaklings, and few aspens grow much over forty feet or so.

It seems a nervous, anxious tree, always quaking, trembling, set in motion by the slightest breeze, fluttering its small egg-shaped leaves, a tree altogether too delicate and possessed by too much sensibility.

Still, the aspens are young trees with young vigor; they will crowd in and be the first to grow after a forest fire, moving in on scarred blackened soils with their hordes of slim saplings. The perpetual adolescent is also the soil-conserving, soil-restoring hero.

Now in September, the straight pale trunk, papery brown and greenish white, glows under a halo; persistent trembling leaves catch and reflect the sun and keep its color alive.

September 18

Deer run more quietly in the woods now, in most parts of the country, and those deer living in forests peripheral to national parks may run there to find sanctuary.

The deer is a game animal, and game arouse controversy and folklore and suspicion. Are there more deer, fewer deer? Game wardens, the referees, take a head count, while the deer, knowing in their bones that their population wins no favors, run scared.

Deer, having been around so long and developed into so many species—seven in North America, with a large number of races, varying from the great Alaska moose to the small deer of chaparral-covered California—seem perhaps too familiar. No one thinks too much of killing deer, who have the manageable look of domestic cattle herds; pioneer settlers matter-of-factly killed deer for food and it is still considered sport to kill a deer.

Deer are hardly endangered; part of the game is to keep the players alive in sufficient numbers. Some of the reported figures seem heavily inflated. Remnants of once-great elk herds live in the national parks, and fewer deer romp in the meadows to delight watching hikers.

The white-tailed deer is commonly seen, a slender engaging creature with modest vegetarian habits and bright alert eyes. Shy of man, still deer will readily learn who is a friend, waiting at doorsteps for a handout. Independent and solitary in the summer, it gathers in cooperative herds during the winter to keep paths open.

The white tail, flag of truce, leaps and flutters at every bound. In autumn, the glowing summer coat is still rusty red, but soon will change to the gray of winter. The buck is a casual lover; he will take only one mate at a time but quickly tires of her. People have frequently come across a fawn lying alone, spotted coat looking like sunlight dappling the forest floor. In a sentimental misunderstanding nurtured on Bambi folklore, such young deer are often rescued, to their sorrow and ultimate death. The fawn has not been abandoned; the doe will return when she has finished her browsing.

Indians hunted and killed deer, not just for food but for every useful bit of the body. The hunter's attitude was pragmatic, but he did not kill indiscriminately or for fun; the deer was useful in a hundred ways. In contrast, the cheerful blunt brutality of the Eskimos as they slaughter seals or hang dogs (for their fur) seems a good-natured, mindless insouciance. In an unloving environment, the Eskimo does not seem able to comprehend any pain that does not happen to him personally.

A game animal—like a pet—is a luxury. Few people kill today for venison or any animal meat, but the language and attitude reflect the concept; the Fish and *Game* Department is in charge of wildlife that is often scarce or nearly extinct. That deer are "managed" is euphemism supreme.

Meanwhile, the uncooperative deer forget the rules, seem to forget it's all a game, and run for their lives.

September 19

After two or three hundred years, faint traces of path still climb and turn in the hills where the Indians walked. Sometimes these paths lead to obscure caves where the Indians painted on rock. Gradually the paintings fade and the trails themselves are eroded and brush-covered. In woods, no trails; forests have no memories and are continually growing, filling the forest floor.

A September day is an opportunity to walk Indian fashion in the woods. Follow a game trail that begins deceptively easy and obvious, and then shifts and changes and loses itself. Indians followed routes made by deer and small animals, because animals cleverly choose the easiest of routes leading to water, avoiding rock cliffs and dense brush.

On the right kind of September day, a human on an old animal/Indian trail finds his mood changing. September has a primitive look and feel, unhurried; there is only the urgent command to the senses to listen, be quiet, absorb the forest world itself in its dimness and stillness. Deeper in the woods there is no view out to hills or sky but only the immediate living trees and brush. In this close, shy darkness, the human mood shifts and becomes less sure of itself, less pompous in its belief that the world was made for or is even accessible to human pleasures.

Walking Indian fashion is walking in silence. Only men who creep soundlessly in the forest will hear the forest: crack and rustle of leaves and twigs, the dry, thin sounds of limbs, a bird with a voice like a bicycle bell, gentlest of wind on the still day.

Only a man walking with his eyes all around his head will catch the glimpse of fox, or get close enough to deer to see their eyes, to see the snake, mellow as bark, curled on a warm rock, taking in the last afternoon heat. Wild animals are shy of direct stares and are seen best when a man appears to be looking somewhere else.

Walking Indian fashion is stopping now and then to eat berries hanging ripe as deeply blue as the darkening sky, smelling the pungent mold-mix of the rich forest floor, feeling the occasional web that still hangs across the path to brush the face.

Indians revered the forest and its trees because they felt life literally breathing and pulsing in every tree, every leaf; for this reason, they would stand against a tree to draw strength from it. To walk like an Indian is to walk quietly, without disturbance, and feel some of that life pouring out to the passerby, an exchange—private and subtle as breath—between human and the nonhuman.

September 21

September belongs to: caterpillars, wasps, flies, spiders, mites. Crickets, chirping day and night, make the dry, astringent music of September.

Second broods of butterflies and moths make their appearance. Woolly bear caterpillars are in a hurry now, seeking a suitable winter retreat.

A last chance for field butterflies, clinging to brush, too cold to escape. Grasshoppers leap and bound in their prissy mechanical way, exuberant in an hour of reprieve, as the few hours of allotted sun still warm their bodies.

Spiders hang webs everywhere; these will be glistening air-castles in morning dew. Occasionally here a dusty miller moth may make his escape by forfeiting some of his dusty wing scales—small price to pay for a little more of life.

Yellowjacket wasps have constructed their paper nests underground, and in the sunshine look for food.

Autumn chill in the air, and time running out, but the smaller members of the world make the most of it, and the crickets continue to rasp—fiddlers for the dance.

September 22

In bright sunset colors the pheasant is the color of fall. The cock is vividly dressed; his hen is a passive brown. Not a native bird (the pheasant was imported from China, Japan, and other parts of Asia), it has adapted well to America, showing a liking for summer-hot valleys and cold winters.

Popular target for sportsmen, the bird often waits concealed till someone is almost upon him before he flies off with a great thrust of wings. Like quail, pheasants have strong family habits, and will parade across a country road, docile as a *Saturday Evening Post* cover. In farmlands, pheasants winter in haystacks, strawpiles, accommodating to man's provisions.

In a "good" year, one in which grain is plentiful and hunters scarce, pheasants will eat companionably in the yard with chickens.

September 23

The first day of autumn. The days and nights are now in almost equal balance, light against the dark. Autumn, officially marked by the calendar, has placed its own sign on the land, in frost and leaf fall, or wine-reddened sky at late afternoon. An ambiguity to the display of brilliant leaves against newly exposed hills, but the sign is unmistakable.

Now is the time to think of: bicycling, walking in the woods, a last picnic on the beach—and also to think of: catching up on reading, taking a night class, making a quilt.

The harvest is in. The land prepares for winter; it is a time for taking stock and making plans. Autumn appeals to a melancholy sense in man which recognizes the shortness of far-away youth, the hardly-to-be-counted pause of summer, the hurrying rush toward maturity and its end consequence, death.

Halfway through the cycle, the landscape glows, and autumn is a gift; it is also a chilly time of reckoning.

September 24

John Muir called him the "squirrel of squirrels." He is a leaping, bounding, chattering gambol of energy and fury, half-flying, using his broad yellow-fringed tail partly for balance; a few more inches shoulder thrust would give him the right to fly.

The Douglas squirrel is acrobat supreme, but with a comic's style; he can act with beseeching clownishness, ingratiatingly appearing to chatter-beg handouts from picnickers. He can also turn instantly cross-tempered, changing from a sweet-eyed mendicant to a scolding, tongue-whipping hothead ready to argue with every other animal in the forest.

Hoarder, the *douglassi* leaves his pinecones in hollow logs or in springs—long-range investments, for the cones will stay fresh for years. Kitchen middens of pinecone scales atop stumps mark a record of his activities. He will also eat nuts and fungi; he is redolent of turpentine.

He was named for David Douglas, a Scotsman botanist who identified the species about 1825 near the Columbia River. Olive-brown and orange-bellied, he is hard to spot 200 feet high in a pine tree, but gives himself away with abandoned leaps and warbling calls—a furry mammal who acts like a bird.

September 25

Barometer of September is one species of the earthstar, a kind of puffball that foretells wet weather if its star points open. Closed points augur continued dry days.

Mushrooms and fungi are abundant now in the woods, the odd obscure candles of the forest floor. A play of dim light in the forest shadows reveals odd, intriguing beauty; the oyster mushroom on stumps and trunks, the rain-hatted *Hydnum*, cloudy puffballs, the oriental-looking destroying angel, lavender-masked *Tricholoma*.

Some fungi—bright orange on a rotting log—have a gross, squat look; others seem delicate and pallid, invalids of dark and moist places. Sea-shaped and colored are the coral mushrooms, branching fungi of pastels in pink, yellow, and violet. Some of the more picturesque are lethal; some of the most grotesque are totally harmless.

Ghostly substance on decaying leaves or wood in damp shade: the slime molds. The viscous slippery mass is a body of naked protoplasm. Unlike other plants, the molds lack chlorophyll, and get their nourishment from the organic substances on which they live. Oddly enough, this least attractive of plants is extremely sensitive to light; lingering in the dampness and darkness while in its vegetative state, it actually begins to move when about to produce spores, and creeps—amoeba fashion—toward sunlight and higher dryer spots.

September 26

Rains now have a cool weight. It seems to rain more often and steadily; rains last longer and are chillier. If it rains all day, the spattered earth is a rebuke and inconvenience. After placid August, rain is a reminder of boots and storm windows and the encumbrances of winter.

Rainwater is a gift, however, and a reminder of earth's essential abundance. Some native tribes in various parts of the world still dance in naked joy in the rain.

Use rainwater to water house plants; some coddled plants sit in apathy and after receiving rainwater react in astonishing fresh growth and greenness, as freely as wild things. Rainwater even makes a good shampoo. Windows washed with rainwater sparkle more alluringly than with any application of chemical sprays.

Rain, a softer water, is a carrier perhaps of fewer minerals but more bounty. After a rainstorm, bird crews descend on the ground, the clean-up gang, retrieving seeds and dislodged insects. A drop of rain, standing on a leaf, is a miniature viewer which reveals astonishing colors and textures. After the days of dryness, rain returns, and the freshened world, even as the pace toward autumn quickens, seems glowing and revived.

September 27

THE UNTRAVELED WORLD

Fewer crowds now in Yosemite Valley (and in other mountain areas of the country) and the granite walls are the least-visited; two figures begin the long climb up El Capitan.

Not too many people travel here—famous names like Royal Robbins, Yvon Chouinard, a handful of the young and ambitious. These climbs seem astonishing, but also impractical; what is the purpose of these one- to two-day ascents? Little virgin soil remains in America, and often it is actually virgin—or at least little-traveled rock.

Impossible to climb in midsummer when the rock scalds the fingers and heat scorches the throat and a climber clings like a dead leaf to the impossible wall. With the cooler days of September the climbers begin their visits to the little traveled world.

A few feet may make the difference between a well-plotted route and original exploration.

The history of rock climbing has evolved full circle from the early unencumbered scrambles, accomplished on little more than spit and daring, to the engineering feats aided by bong-bongs and an assortment of hardware; now the cycle is swinging back. Chocks and rope for protection, but the route is unmarked, and the climber ultimately is testing only his own skill and determination. He calls this climbing clean; it is a purer adventure, closer to the spirit of first mountaineering, when there is little iron or equipment between the embrace of man and rock.

Rock climbing done by an expert looks both easy and slow, like sinuous underwater movements. The leader never seems to hurry—indeed he cannot—but as the minutes and then the hours pass, he has progressed painstakingly upwards.

A good rock climber looks as graceful as a ballet dancer and has the same suggestion of suppleness and strength. Someone like Gaston Rebuffat is wiry and compact; women often become good climbers by practicing an innate delicacy of balance and movement. Fearless? Probably the best climbers have the most tingling respect for the long drop beneath. Experts keep in shape by jogging, hanging on doorsills, clutching rubber balls for finger strength.

Only one man moves at a time, and the second must often wait out long stretches on rock spaces that would hardly accommodate a whisker. First maxim in climbing: the leader does not fall. When he reaches a secure spot (room for a whisker more), he adopts a Buddha-calm stance and belays the second who climbs up to join him.

Air and rock. The ping of a hammer. Nothing more. The valley is a long ways down. A little crowd of impatient watchers who stand confusedly looking at men who choose such odd attitudes and pastimes. At night, if these outrageous acrobats must bivouac, they lie in hammocks, munching snacks and drinking water. Thirst is the constant companion.

In darkness, only air and rock, and the spatter of stars. Morning is knife-cold and the shadow of the rock peak lies bulky on the valley floor. Now the men are stiff and uncomfortable, having had sleep in little more than fits and starts and such dreams as visit travelers in an untraveled world.

Where everything is vertical, no running about or much stamping of feet. The frailty of the human body and the harsh strength of granite are in direct and immediate exchange.

Slowly the rock warms and the men move on. Here and there a fragment of brown lichen in a crevice. Occasionally the leader calls; he deviates from the route—that pure vision held in his eye—when an overhang or a sheer stretch forces him aside. A wrinkle in the rock is a toehold. A crack a quarter of an inch deep is a handhold.

Air and rock—air as flimsy as breath, with nothing to hang onto if a man fell and went crashing and careening down. Rock so straight and silent it seems to lean massively forward pushing the men out. Rock climbers learn almost at once to stand upright; to lean against the unwelcoming rock is to become giddy and confused with shaking knee and grunting breath.

Now, the summit is anticlimax, an acre of throw-away cans and bottles and kleenex and the loud cheerful voices of tourists.

The travelers have returned.

September 28

Indian summer comes upon the countryside, the last lingering afterglow of summer's radiance. It is a reprieve only, a postponement of the harsh earnestness of winter, and no one takes seriously its playful mood; yet a coin-gold September afternoon is relaxed and benign, and the earth seems to have relented.

The day's edges are blurred. Morning mists, cool and thin, are dim and separate on the horizons, and the twilight is a blue unsubstantial vapor, quickly gone. Clouds like smoke drift at a leisured pace. But the air, in contrast, has a crispness; the air tightens and chills as the earth slowly cools and the daylength shortens. September is not even a pause, really, as the land hurries toward its winter appointments.

September is a pageant of color, last surprising firm statements of authority: apples redden, peaches are red-gold in sunny ripeness, along stone walls and in shady arbors grapes are smoky blue-purple. Leaves become the most vivid of colors—yellow, red, the blazing primaries. The harvest colors are the most spectacular, just before leaves turn brittle and the fruit is gathered. Goldenrod is a primal yellow—an advancing tide on the edges of meadows.

For many Indian tribes, the September days were a time of hurry in that brilliant-decorated haze, gathering berries and nuts against approaching autumn and winter. For animals, a last chance to feast on fruits and berries in the time of plenty. The birds and animals may not be particularly aware of the colors at all—food selection is a complex process—but the entire landscape, in some areas, is as brilliant as a poster display; fields and woods are nature's billboards proclaiming last chance.

September 29

In September, the chaparral is brittle and dry in the Los Padres National Forest in central California. It has not rained since March, and the manzanita and the tall harsh yucca wait for the beginning of the rainy season. It is a frail gray-brown world here, an old, old world, the hard core and veins of the mountains showing through in deep-slashed ridges and canyons and slopes of bare rocks. The bright blue sky is like a hard crust. Then a stroke of black in the sky, gradually growing larger, the California condor.

At one time, the condor had immense room to roam, as befits his enormous size; in Washington and in Oregon in the 1800s the great scavenger traveled unhampered in his lonely flight. His declining days are cramped; two tiny reserves in the Los Padres National Forest are the condor's final sanctuary.

Perhaps forty or so of the birds remain; it is difficult to count condors, who are shy and distrustful of man, obstinately clinging to life in this last wild area. Condors, who produce only one young bird every other year will, if startled or frightened, abandon the eggs or fledglings on the sandstone ledges. In captivity the condor does not breed at all. Efforts to protect the bird are probably remarkably futile in the long run; the sanctuaries are too near the accessible trails and motorbikes and guns. Condors prefer silence and long empty stretches of hollow sky where they can survey the canyons below for dead animals.

Living on carrion, the condor is himself an unlikeable bird, almost grotesque in his appearance and habits; any national campaign mounted to save the condor will have to do much retouching to appeal to the country's imagination. Huge funereal black body, scrubby orange head, a brutal beak; the condor is hardly winsome.

In size alone, he is vulnerable as a target with a wingspan of ten feet or more. To get such huge bodies airborne condors run on the ground, wings flapping, several yards. Once in the air, however, the condor is capable of flights of thirty to forty miles an hour, and he can soar for an hour without flapping his wings.

He searches the ravines; forest fire is an enemy but a blaze also clears the brush and exposes carrion to easy view.

A long life, slow-geared to bigness; young birds do not fly for five months, and do not mature until five or six years old. Some naturalists claim a lifespan of forty years for the condor.

The birds fly, usually in a pair, in magnificent, easy deliberation, perfectly at balance in the dry hot air, a lonely team of skillful hunters.

Preoccupied with death, looking for the dead, the condor is unaware that his own days are being marked off one by one.

September 30

THE NURSE

A walk in the woods brings the realization that the forest is at work, in the continual cycle of destruction and rebuilding.

A falling tree has hit the ground, and the forest begins the labor of turning it into soil and new life. The attack starts: bacteria and fungi weaken and break down the fibers; lichen and mosses grow in the decaying, crumbling wood as the fallen log becomes a moist shelter.

The fallen tree becomes a nurse log, supporting the intertwining roots of birch and rhododendron. As the young trees grow, the log completely rots away beneath the arching tentacles of roots.

Decay returns minerals and adds new life to the soil. In this rich habitat spruce and hemlock seeds will germinate and sprout. Soon, the seedlings take root, and in this moist bounteous nursery, new trees begin life.

Autumn:
Twilight of the Year

October 1

Patterns for October: flame-shaped, flame-colored leaves on the move; Indian sketches of life drawn boldly on rocks, simplified to the bare essentials or figured in high-riding fancies; trees twisted by the wind.

October 2

October is cooler, as the sun's rays strike the earth at more of a slant. The temperature is still mild and frisky, but the air has a nip in it, and the occasional day of rain is decidedly chill. Not an unpleasant month—at the beginning October is still nut-brown and winsomely beautiful with decorated trees, and the sky is blue; white thin clouds race; children accomplish a grand bit of noise on the way home from school. Towards twilight, the skies have the elegant delicacy of parchment, and long, slanting shadows deepen to smudged violet; there is an air of frailty and impermanence to this span between summer and winter. Sumacs add brilliant colors: reds, yellows, bronze golds, even bringing creeping color up the stern scree and gravel slopes of mountains. Oaks are softest ruddy colors of crimson and magenta, and the delicate beeches and birches are limpid shades of gray and pale yellow; leaves are translucent. Shock of brittle scarlet: the poison ivy in shadowy recesses. Wild aster and goldenrod are still in bloom. The air is clear, and quieter than it has been; many of the insects are gone.

October 4

The day of Saint Francis of Assisi.

Probably the most appealing of saints, and a man whose undeniable charm seems to mean something different to every person. Preaching (and living) a message of poverty and humility, he is also the only saint associated with nature.

The familiar stance, preaching to the birds, speaks clearly to modern man. This was not the moody monk, or the fevered mystic, but the man who had renounced the world and continued in love with it: "My brother birds, you ought always to praise and love your Creator, who has given you feathers for clothing, wings for flight, and all that you have need of. He has given you a dwelling in the purity of the air, though you sow not, neither do you reap." This began a new strain in Christianity, and one that has persisted here and there, a gentler, more joyful assertion of the spirit in Brother Ass. Today, however, many of those birds have vanished in Italy, and linger only in sanctuaries such as the woods round the Franciscan Carceri, guarded by the memory of Francis. The gentle saint did not speak only to birds. The town of Gabbio was threatened by a wolf pack that destroyed flocks and killed men. Alone, Saint Francis visited a wolf's lair, and returned, followed by a meekly trotting wolf who for two years was the pet and respected member of the city.

The story tells more than just the human need for miracles, for strange and powerful control over wild animals. Saint Francis re-creates the myth of man in nature, the loving and coexisting resident of

Eden. The wolf is the free and wild spirit, and Saint Francis calls forth the deep myths of the man/animal heart. A romantic, Saint Francis could argue for the sternest of discipline and cruel rigors, even while he gloried in life and all its manifestations, all the baffling joyous textures of nature. He overthrew the limitations, like another saint who was to follow, John Muir.

Ironically, the Franciscan order in the 1700s established a chain of twenty-one missions in California, founded by the zealot Father Junipero Serra, each a stiff day's march apart, devoted to the cause of converting the Indians. Here the Indians were taught to pray, but also to render tallow and make candles and weave. Plunged into rough work and harsh discipline, living in damp, chill buildings and given a meager and unfamiliar diet, the Indians quickly succumbed.

The gentle Indians who had lived in nature were in effect slain by the Franciscan fathers. The statue of Saint Francis broods in the olive-shaded courtyard: "Lord, make me an instrument of Thy peace . . ."

October 5

> With no bird singing
> The mountain is yet more still.
>
> *–Zen saying*

Late-departing birds migrate in October—the sharp-shinned hawk, red-tailed and pigeon hawks, thrushes and wood warblers, the endangered peregrine falcon.

Flocks of chipping sparrows and catbirds depart, and grackles pass overhead.

The insect eaters go as the days cool and sharpen and insects go underground for the winter. Termite ants migrate down into the soil, and beetles retire for the long night, underneath stones and logs. The sounds of the crickets dwindle. Bees vanish as the queens search for retreats; a few butterflies, inconspicuous in color, remain.

October birds are seed-eaters, in the main. Winter residents will be the nuthatches and the woodpeckers, and the blue jay—louder, raspier than ever, taking over nearly unoccupied territory. Blue jays, with no respect or compunction for other birds, fall silent only at the approach of a great hawk, and if one of their number is snatched up, will circle back to hold a noisy wake.

Many snakes have moved to winter dens; frost drives away frogs and salamanders. Still, the life in stream and pond continues much as it has, and will until the water cools sharply. Brook trout are moving upstream to their spawning ground.

October 6

The weather is anticyclonic; there are occasional sharp clashes between the still warm Atlantic and the cold Arctic, but in general October remains the iron hand in the velvet glove. The days are frequently blue-bland and mild; until the nippy dusk it seems that Indian summer is lingering. Shredded white clouds float in a peaceful sky; a haze in the air comes from burning leaves and the dust of dry autumn. The rains are not yet, generally, too heavy or too long-lasting. But at higher elevations snow is falling; in the mountains winter comes swiftly.

October 7

Corn was the frontier food. Corn could be boiled, fried, roasted. Ground, it was a versatile meal, appearing in breakfast mush, breads, pudding. Baked with milk and eggs, it was a hearty custard.

The staple traveled with the pioneers, and the test of a new homesite was, Will it grow corn?

A corn husking bee was an autumn festivity, as people gathered to strip the ears of the dry leaves. Each man selected a partner; finding a red ear meant the privilege of a kiss. After all the ears were husked, the fiddle was brought out and the harvesters danced the rest of the night away.

October 8

October is a matron having her last fling, with gaudy leaves in her hair, and a high-spirited glint of midday sunlight in her eyes. But the matron earth cools, and composes itself to sit for a family portrait in sepia. Leaves fall and acquire a bronze patina. The matron becomes discreet.

Soon the trees will have a chaste look, with the leafless simplicity that must have appealed to the guilt-ridden Puritans, who foresaw retribution and deprivation in the gray days approaching. As the leaves fall, further vistas open, and the crowding hills look closer. Fields are bare, and straggler zinnias droop; some neighbor flowers browned and died in the first frost. The passions have cooled.

October 9

Hard to find, but bravely in bloom in chill October, the bottle gentian. The flowers are a subdued blue, and tightly closed, like small sealed bottles. The plants are well hidden in moist, lush growth along ditches or roadside banks.

Gentiana andrewsii bears two distinguished names: Henry C. Andrews, the English painter of flowers, and King Gentian, who ruled Illyria (Shakespeare's *Twelfth Night* country, now Albania and Yugoslavia). King Gentian, according to Pliny, discovered medicinal qualities in gentian root. The bottles remain closed, sitting in a frame of close-circled narrow leaves; it takes a persistent bumblebee to drive into the folded tip of the flower for pollen.

October 10

In the Colorado Rockies, great stands of aspen trees bear ugly black scars. The trunks have been chewed by elk. The spectacle is the result of man's taking over the animals' natural feeding grounds, and forcing them to seek marginal foods.

October 11

THE BALANCE OF NATURE

A great deal has been written about the balance of nature, which has a pleasing sound—on paper. It is perfectly true that ecological animal/plant communities are complex webs of interdependence, of checks and controls; yet these are not communities of mutual aid nor always even forbearance. Eden has its dark side.

Animal eats plant, or animal; the life form grows as nourishment for another life form. In the end, all life exists on other forms of life, and death is the sure basis of life. Viewed with a dispassionate eye, man's activities seem no more than the bustle of the ant or bee colony. Wars come along to check the population explosion, or drugs invent new diseases. Race riots or youth demonstrations or the Kent State brutality kill bystander and participant alike; man eats his fellow man, too. Despite the ritual conciliatory sacrifices of such inanities as capital punishment, in which a few paltry and expendable Negroes or Chicanos are slaughtered, the gods are never appeased.

Men believe themselves to live outside the cage of instinct. Actually, they are driven and possessed, riding the runaway horses of emotion and drive; in other words, men live instinctively.

Pessimistically, nature is seen as nothing more than a start/stop operation. Animals cooperate—there are structured societies of insects, and the help an animal often gives another—but the instinct to kill is in the genes. For every pleasure, pain; for every growth, retreat.

So far, in nature, on this planet, a roughly fifty-fifty balance. In one way of looking at it, nature never gets off the ground. Species come and go; so-called higher life forms are more complex, but not necessarily more enduring. Men keep searching for a positive note in this blind, disorderly process and invent religions, but close their eyes to the obvious: the watchmaker has bad luck.

Possibly, no order or choice exists. All creatures die, but equally, they have no choice but to live.

The garter snake swallows the frog, the Venus's-flytrap swallows the bee. On the other hand, the blue jay brings food to a crippled jay, the elk with a wild look in his bloodshot eyes charges off to find a mate, the surly pugnacity of the chicken keeps the pecking order intact and the egg is laid. The viceroy butterfly "imitates" the monarch and saves its own life by appearing inedible; coyotes hunt in efficient relay teams. Men, when not fighting, compose poems and send a Titan to the stars.

October 12

Now is the time to plant bulbs: tulips, daffodils, hyacinths. Colorless and squat, looking much like the crude eggs they actually are, the bulbs go into the ground (not yet frozen and resistant), there to take root, and during the long dormant months of winter prepare for that early appearance.

The surest sign of spring is the bulb planted on a chilly October day.

October 13

On Columbus Day, 1966, a windstorm raced up the coast from northern California to Oregon and Washington. The weather had been bland in temperature, October mild, but it had rained heavily, and the ground was wet and sodden.

As the storm appeared, radio announcements warned of high winds, but few were seriously alarmed; fall and winter storms often brought gales and downpour to the green and damp Pacific Northwest.

Columbus and his sailors had been justifiably frightened by the trade winds of the North Atlantic, saved by the westerlies that blew east across America. Now, on a settled coast, few suspected the violence of the coming wind. Air is actually a moving sea—the interplay of air between the cold icecaps and the warm tropics—and as the earth spins, it drags behind a moving sea of air. Storms arise when moving winds clash.

As the great winds ran north, they spoke in a whining urgency. In Oregon, in Portland and Salem, people watched great trees fall, pulled out of the wet, resistless ground. In Seattle, people stood at their windows, watching, and jumped back when branches hit the glass. Trees came crashing down. A madrona tree, a couple of hundred years old, tons in weight, struck the ground between a house and carport. In the darkness, power lines fell and lay writhing and sputtering, and lights went out in the city. On Puget Sound, waves leaped and buckled in response to the wind. Cars pulled off to the side of the road, and people gazed at the visible wind. A storm has a great loudness; in the silence of stilled radios and voices, the steady hoarse roar of the wind.

Finally the storm moved on and blew itself out, and silence came. In that welcome silence, there was an initial exhilaration, but it was three or four days before power was restored everywhere, and people looked in dismay at what a single night's wind had accomplished. Trees in the state capitol grounds at Salem lay uprooted and spilled; barns, their sides blown off, teetered crazily in fields. The sudden storm, like a blunt, impersonal affront, seemed rude and unreasonable, an unpremeditated, witless violence.

In the forests, not so much havoc, trees closely supporting each other with their network of roots in the firmer ground, and close branches, muffled the wind's force; only in cities and towns the look of bleakness and devastation. Damage, like beauty, is in the eye of the beholder. Now the silence was replaced by the whine of the power saw as the work of cutting and hauling away of logs began.

There is something satisfying to a great storm (if the onlooker escapes its power); it is proof of the living force of nature, earth and air still on the move.

October 14

THE KEY

After a light rain, winged seedpods drop from the Norway maple tree, lying like keys on the lawn in scattered profusion, additional evidence of nature's generosity, which always provides in excess—more than margin for the unexpected. Children used to make wishes on these frail brown keys found on lawns, and it was considered lucky to have one come fluttering down directly to a waiting hand. In a sense, the children were right; the seed is the key to everything.

October 15

The rock paintings of the American Indian continue to baffle observers. The colors will fade before the researchers can come up with an answer—why did the Indians paint? What do the drawings mean?

In shadowy caves, remote up a canyon wall screened by trees, the drawings that are absurd and beautiful excite and entertain, but the essential meaning eludes, and leaps away.

A sun circle, in red and green. A scarlet pinwheel. A salamander. Leaping stick figures with headdresses that have the look of premedieval angels. A cow on wheels. Red ochre lasts; the blues and greens from serpentine are more scarce, and vulnerable to light. Wind and rain erosion take away drawings and leave only dim and indecipherable markings.

Many theories have been offered on the paintings: Nothing more than casual graffiti. (A log placed by a cave entrance soon acquires its share of scrawled names.) Religious or magical drawings, made by the shaman in his hideaway. The artists composed under the influence of gypsum weed with its known psychedelic effect. The figures were drawn to bring good luck in hunting and fishing. The Indians exhorted the gods of the weather in rain and sun symbols. The Indians painted portraits of their deities (a swordfish was supposedly worshipped). The Indians simply drew what they saw (later paintings occasionally show a ship, or an anchor, or a deer; there is a man on horseback).

As many theories as there are paintings—but all full of large holes. Occasionally the artistry is detailed and perfectionist; just as often it is little more than crude finger dabblings. If Indians drew what they saw, their vision was apparently erratic and confused; some figures seem bizarre, a curious bestiary of haloed stickmen and aquatic creatures that appear about to take flight. Probably no Indian worshipped a swordfish, which was simply another manifestation of a democratic and abundant spirit.

Investigators go about their work seriously, measuring, photographing, analyzing the lichen and rock and associated ecofacts (shells, snails) to determine possible dates of the paintings. Vandals are often just as much in earnest; coming unexpectedly upon cave art, they have riddled the paintings with bullet holes or written their own names across a figure or a starlike symbol (names have powerful, magic meanings, though modern man, like primitive man, seldom draws his own face; the soul might escape). This would seem to be a particularly graceless assertion of the territorial imperative; man marks his cave, even if there only one day on a jackrabbit-hunting expedition.

On an October day, in the stillness, a sheltered cave seems haunted; the drawings look newly made, and the artist may just have stepped around the corner. Here and there in the rock, huge birds that look mythical, a dancing stick figure carrying a ponderous headdress.

Professor Herbert Kunz, foremost authority on European

rock art, has suggested that the paintings represent concepts, not things. If this is correct, the amusing delicate figures and the bold suns are the portraits of good and evil, the famine and the longing, the mysteries that pull and twitch at man's mind as they always have through the centuries. If they could be thus deciphered, the paintings would chart equally the primitive and the modern quest.

Serious work, for a fact, to find facts in these paintings (fully as abstract and as troubling as any Pollock or Tobey or Albers).

In the dim cave, a fancy, antennae-eared bear rolls a wheel. This is art with a profound message: the world is funny and to be taken lightly, with a vision of the perpetual whimsy of fate. The American Indian, at least until the white man came, had a sense of humor.

October 17

Owls screech more often as the autumn nights lengthen. Wisdom is often associated with sinister-looking or -sounding creatures—the serpent, the raven—and the tremulous wail of the owl, loud in the darkness, has credited it with more sagacity than it may actually possess.

In the night, the owl's voice, actually not a screech but a plaintive shiver of sound, has a melancholy fierceness: in the South, folks shiver in response when they hear the cry and say that someone will die or some dire trouble is about to befall.

Trouble befalls on mice and rats, snails and even a small bird; the owl, poor of vision by day and made irascible by sunlight, is a busy nocturnal hunter. The owl is disliked by other birds, who may scold briskly at the entrance of the owl's hideout—a hollow in a tree—and even give quarreling chase.

Like the barn owl, its larger cousin, the screech owl is partial to the habitats of man, and will often choose to nest near houses and barns, even on accommodating ledges. Small—nine or ten inches—the bird has a big-eyed face and scowling brows; it looks perpetually disturbed, with a cross expression to match its trembling cry. Some folks are sure the owl cries miserably, "Ooooooh oooooh wooooe is me." Wisely, the owl says little more. A person in a disgruntled and complaining mood is said to be "owly."

October 19

In 1972, American gun business was big business—over half a billion dollars.

Many bullets were bought to kill animals. Organizations which oppose hunting or needless slaughter are variously called heavy breathers, bleeding hearts, and little old ladies in tenny runners. Concerned with animal lives, devoted to the cause of protecting animal life, of nurturing an ethic of gentleness and fair play in the treatment of animals, these organizations are also called humanitarian.

October 20

In the desert, the saguaro cactus waits for winter rains. Here, rain comes infrequently but heavily, and the desert plants must drink and store what they can, all at once, when the opportunity comes. Small cactuses have a reptilian, somnolent look; the ribbed giant saguaro is a thorny and wizened thing, a skeleton with uplifted horns.

The life of the saguaro has one aim: the conservation of moisture. Shrunken and wrinkled after dry weeks, it waits, like a water vessel to be filled. In a flood-rain, an old plant—perhaps fifty feet tall and two hundred years old—may take in a ton of water.

October 21

Some of the most beautiful trees in the world live just at timberline in the forest stands and the barren upper zones where summer pays only a fleeting visit. These are short, slanted trees, stunted in growth, standing in thin random groups or alone, in battered, leaning, crouching postures. Driven and bent by wind, such trees appear small and spindly, and may be a century old or more, eking out a skimpy existence in unnourishing rock and soil.

Still, these trees have an angular beauty, repeating the shapes of wind patterns. Hemlock, fir and pine grow in these inhospitable places high on the mountains, surviving year after year the wind's buffeting; the most photographed tree in the world is the rough-shaped Jeffrey pine in Yosemite, the true picture of endurance. On the slopes of Mount Hood at the edge of perpetual snow, stand alpine firs, thin-trunked and spiky little drab gray-green trees, a cheerless and dispossessed group of individuals still hanging on. Life forms in nature tolerate and accommodate, if they are to last; the secret of immortality is adaptability.

October 23

RUFFLES AND FLOURISHES

A walker in the woods strolls in silence, the trees are wrapped in quietness. Suddenly an explosion of banging, vibrating wings as a great brown bird launches skyward.

The ruffed grouse is a disconcerting bird with its penchant for last-second exits, and its heady alarums. Liking woods and dense brush where it can hide or quickly find safe cover, it is an inconspicuous bird despite its size (sixteen to nineteen inches), resembling an overgrown barnyard hen.

A ruff of green-black feathers decorates the shoulders of the bird, particularly showy on the male. A timid bird, but ostentatious in its announcements; it is the male that drums out his song of love (and of warning to rival males at all times of the year), and a particular loud, drumming sound on a quiet October afternoon. The drumming is done by the wings beating against the air and may go on for several minutes. Hikers can approach quite close before the sound stops. The drummer finds a stump or log for a platform, and begins the performance: a slow series of thumps that gradually increase in speed, building to a heavy hollow roll and ending in a great sonorous flourish. The air seems still and expectant when the sound ends; soon the drumming begins again. Hen grouse, less vocal, are inordinately protective mothers, good at playing the broken-wing game to divert attention from the chicks.

Not afraid of hard weather, the ruffed grouse stays on in winter through much of the country. As the snow falls and deepens, the grouse sprouts tiny hairlike fingers on its toes. The delicate marks of these fringed toes record the drummer's marches in the muffled forest.

October 25

On an October night, a full moon is a beautiful sight; now the sense of mystery and wonder is restored. Gold and round and perfect, this is the symbol of the harvest brought in, the successful hunt, the gathering night. The moon is for conjecture and longing, once again the spell-binding medallion of uncharted space and unthinkable mysteries. On an October night the infinite universe is a possibility.

On October 13 the planet Jupiter comes into opposition with the sun and moves back into the evening sky. Biggest in the solar system, fiercely red, Jupiter has the look of challenge.

Greatest benefit of space travel to man, not the spinoff benefits of technology, or the chest-thumping assertions of colonial superiority, but the sights and words that will come back from the travelers, the input from the outer edges. On a shrunken planet cage in the galactic outposts, man's brain has evolved little from the Neanderthal; the new stimuli of space-growth may trigger the renewed growth of the human brain. The mind too needs space to grow in.

October 26

Leaves burning, brush burning—these are the friendly suburban and rural smells of autumn. (Ecologists should avail themselves of humility and admit to the homely reassurance of the smoke signal.) People are gathering firewood to store against the coming winter. A late afternoon rain starts up, heavier and colder than a shower; householders hurry inside to build a fire. Fireplaces, unused all summer, blaze now with the warm comfort of flame. Fire has always been something to be made a personal possession.

Primitive man may have been frightened of fire, which could burn and destroy, but always was tempted by it; in its light and glow he saw personal power. Adam and Eve may have stolen a burning branch from the Garden of Eden; the tree of knowledge was ablaze. Only one sure distinction can be made between man and other animals: a chimpanzee may paint a picture, but man handles fire.

A good fire is a satisfying accomplishment, a reward at the end of a hard day's work in field or garden, a comforting thing to have in the house, a visible proof of labor.

To provide the much desired warmth and light, a good fire must be carefully built. Kindling and paper are meticulously laid and the great logs are put near at hand. Ashes provide a bed for the logs. A large log is selected to be the backlog, placed well against the back of the fireplace, with a small log balanced on top. In the front, just behind the andirons, goes another log. Kindling is placed between these two guardian logs.

The choice of wood is important: apple is favored; other excellent choices are white oak and hickory, sugar maple, cherry or birch—all good hardwoods. Most woods burn fitfully and sluggishly when green, but ash and pine logs are exceptions. Driftwood, pungent with the salts and minerals of the sea, burns in a bright display of blue and green sea colors.

Fires are of course useful for heat, and the most satisfying meals are those cooked over fireplaces. But the fires' greatest value is in their colors and music; this is the original sound and light show of crackling movement and red and pure yellow flames. Wóods burn with their own special sounds: hickory is musical; chestnut burns in a series of twangy pops.

Good fires should be personally and attentively tended; instinct demands that the firekeeper be close at hand, shifting a log now and then, feeding the fire a placating stick or twig, bringing the consumed back and front logs to the center and replacing them. All this can be done on the pretext of watching for stray sparks.

Long after dark, when the house quiets and its owners go to bed, the fire burns down and dies, but occasionally a log settles and shifts, and a flame like a hand leaps to point upward and draws back. The room is dark, and now the fire is a faint glow, personal and satisfying, like something alive in the room.

October 28

Late in October the brook trout mate. The female sweeps out a deep nest with the dashing motion of her body in the cool and gravelly current. The male watches, and fights off rivals. Now, the rites of courtship, and the female covers the nest with gravel. The eggs will rest here at the stream bottom through winter, to be hatched in the spring. The brook trout is everybody's favorite; it is bred in artificial ponds and in spring-water hatcheries and planted in mountain streams. It is probably the most familiar fish; dark, or brilliantly patterned, it is the "fish of fish" to thousands of anglers. Living originally in cold northern waters, and along the Alleghenies, the fish were a lively ten pounds of catch. Today, overbred and commonplace, most brook trout weigh a pound or less.

Has it ever struck you that the trouts bite best on the Sabbath?

—*James Matthew Barrie*

October 30

THE PERFECT CIRCLE

On the forest floor: layers of leaves, layers of needles, fragments of bark. The leaf mold has a sweet/sour smell where the leaves are blackening and decaying, a slippery slush-slap of sound where the hiker walks. The real stillness of the forest is in its soft leaf rustle. Evergreens intermix with spindly alder and brush and salal, and after the first fall rains, water drips from branches and bush, a pulsebeat of sound.

If the earth were transparent, it would show a vein network of thin outreaching branches perfectly reflecting the upper tree; these are the root feeders that spread out underground. The thrust of the tree is upward; a living tree is supported by dead cells, the heartwood at its center, that was once sapwood, now solidified and pressed by growing cells around it. Against gravity, water is taken up through pale sapwood pipes, in the ingenious process of transpiration through leaves and pores; as water evaporates, a message is sent down the tree to the roots to bring up more water. A tree grows outward in a premeditated living architecture from the heartwood; first the sapwood, then the cambium, the green cells that simultaneously put down rings and grow more bark, then the bark itself. A tree is as mellow as a violin with the twang and give of the earth's resonance in the structure, with hollow cells of flexible cellulose. A towering tree has a tremendous tall craving for water and light.

At its trunk, leaves fall and bark rots; in time this becomes the forest duff, the rich mix of vegetation and moisture and mold, of seed and brush that will be the next tree, the forest to come.

October 31

Halloween used to be called "snap-apple" time. The jack-o'-lantern grinned at the window like the reflected face of the moon.

The night then was still a shivery and scary time; goblins crept out of the woods to share the blue dusk, on a once-a-year trip to the world of living men. Children ran fast between houses to collect their trick-or-treat.

On the eve of All Souls' Day, no one believed in ghosts and ghoulies, but the trees, stripped of leaves, had a spectral look and an owl cried pensively in the shadows. Then, like the Irish, folks did not believe in ghosts, but knew they were there.

The end of October is the haunting time; the ghost of summer gone walks under the last moon.

November 1

   Patterns of November: the brown leaf, turning back to its veined and wired cage-shape; clouds heavy and massed in bulky forms, flying low; shells tossed on the beach; a few leaves hanging yet on the trees and colored like a setting sun.

November 3

   Babies born in November often tend to be aggressive, dominating, sure of their opinions, and are apt to be very bright. Astrology (a kitchen table science compounded in equal parts of supposition and hogwash and hope) claims that human characteristics are determined by the position of the planets at birth.

The other explanation—one that a few scientists are studying—is the influence of weather and season at time of conception.

Humans—like grain, flowers, lizards, or even volcanic rock, for that matter—are subject to the earth's turn, and the play of light and warmth. Conception in March occurs during a time of winds and sun and rain, a restless, burgeoning time; some of that changeable, assertive drive is reflected in a November birth—more often than by chance. Statistics are uncertainties, but the months of October and December produce more than their share of intelligent people.

A baby conceived in November, on the other hand, may arrive in March already possessed of a handicap—an emotional and mental predisposition to oversensitivity, sullenness, brooding, a moody and suspicious outlook on life.

Since man was divested of his supernatural origins, he has been variously called a bad animal, a programed machine, an unused brain, a tool-using predator, an evolutionary experiment. All of these descriptions are true, but overlook the fact that man is an earthbound creature, subject not only to training, conditioning, and heredity, family and cultural traits, but his simple bondage to the earth itself.

This he cannot escape. Man is committed to the earth; he is not a child of the stars, or the sea, or the empty heavens.

A very simple example: the onset of rain means aching bones and rheumatism to a great number of people. Doctors say this is imagination (which merely proves that doctors as a class lack imagination). The reaction is partly physical, partly the heightened sensitivity induced by atmospheric changes. With other people the ache is in the mind, a mood-lowered glumness of anxiety.

People become rapists and killers just before violent windstorms, or the brooding foehn—the warm, dry wind of the mountains. On a drab rainy day in November, people become totally self-centered, broodingly aware of mortality and bills and ailments. A bright spring day exerts a grudging adjustment in a winter-tuned body; people are feckless and unenterprising, gaping at unaccustomed light. This is spring fever. The transient bound of energy that many people experience on a crisp fall day is in part the speeded metabolism of cooler temperatures, and clearer sunlight.

Fog, lingering too long, induces a clammy anxiety, and feelings of indecision and pessimism. Some people crave sunlight, seeming to need it in inordinate quantities. These become the sun worshippers, chasing nonexistent jobs in California, or in old age, settling themselves like schools of dispossessed fish in Florida's hospitable coves. People who live in the sun often become mellower, ripening like fruit, with a lighter, less demanding outlook on life; the hardest adjustment for a farmer from Iowa is to stop taking life's work so seriously. Such people are literally transplants; it is a shock to the root system to move to an alien climate. Thus: the dour and hardworking people of the North, the unambitious South, the restless Westerners (there is a stray suspicion of truth in all these folklore generalities).

A woman wanting a bright and vigorous baby would do well to consult the earth itself, and conceive on a warm spring day, and when the sun and light, as much as any vitamin pill or protein formula, nurture the complex chemical system that is a human being.

November 4

A LIGHT FOR WITCHES

A bright note on November's masked days: the little yellow ribbons of the witch hazel, still hanging on the bare branches of the shrub. A small tree—twenty-five feet in height—the witch hazel is cut down and ground, to be used in cosmetics and lotions for its cool and astringent tang. At midafternoon, dusk is imminent under a close, lowering sky, but the sharp brittle yellow of the familiar shrub is a caution light with a warning: the large black seeds may suddenly be discharged like bullets, shot forth to travel forty or forty-five feet.

November 6

Early November can be mild, with crisp football days and yellow crysanthemums blooming in the garden. Or it can be an undecided brutish time, as the days hurry toward winter.

Earth is cooler, the days shorten; a sunny day gives inexplicable sheen to the nearer-appearing hills. Dusk comes quickly; at five o'clock it is nearly dark. Winter is closing in, the night air has a sharp pinch to it. A gray day follows, heavy and blurred with clouds, and a rainstorm, bearing wind like a whip, sends leaves flying.

November can be changeable, unsettled, or downright unpleasant, but often setting the pattern for weeks ahead. A good

November, some folks say, is a bad sign, as if the earth were a ledger, with so many days of light to be balanced against days of dark, accounts to be settled.

November 7

FROST IS THE VICTOR

Overnight, the earth has changed. The temperature plunged and the first hard frost, sudden and lethal, killed. Flowers have turned hard gray on blackened stalks and sag, as totally crushed as if they had been stoned. The ground is brittle and dark. Frost introduced spaces between bushes, a few leaves and branches snapped under the weight of cold, and empty holes stand between the tall leaning weeds along the road. To the victor, the spoils: ruined flowers, brown grass, the black broken leaves.

November 8

A mud-colored day, clouds like clay, a gray sky heavy and heaving with the threat of storms from the north. At three in the afternoon, with only the slightest trace of wind, the brooding sky seems to hang directly overhead, dropping down steadily closer, and in the clouds, a peculiar tense cast of light: snow! The afternoon darkens, there is a ruffle of wind, the air has a slippery wet feel. But the somber day merges into dusk and nothing has happened; not yet that instant perfect conjoining of temperature and moisture which will provide the first snowfall. This is a dress rehearsal only. November is a month, too, of halting and advance, as the cooling earth turns and wind creaks at the wheel.

November 9

In November, the last of the leaves fall.
On a frosty morning, some of the leaves that have resisted wind and rain drop now as the sun warms the tree, and ice between the

stem of the leaf and the branch melts and snaps. Leaves, like rocks, are subject to the freezing and thawing process. In wind, leaves drop, a swirl of bright, tossed aside color. A few at a time seems the rule, but more perceptibly and faster than the tree greened, the tree becomes bare. Leaves were never mere ornaments. Green, they moved to catch sunlight or to regulate and signal the presence of moisture. Turning to vivid colors, they became useless as mechanisms and served no more purpose in the slower, sealed life of trunk and limb. An ingenious swelling of cells then grew to separate the dead leaf and the tree. This was the literal breaking point, easily snapped by melting frost, or wind. In perfect stillness, leaves will still fall, pushed away by the layer of cells that thrusts outward.

Deciduous trees, fully fleshed in leaves, or bare, are the most obvious—and one of the most satisfying—signs of the seasons. More than anything else, the November stripped trees are proof of winter's approach, the turn of the wheel. But the bare tree, virgin again of growth, remains too a signal of the far-off spring.

November 10

Dark winter mornings like the stone at the door. An inertia to the dawn, which finally emerges, listless and without spark; by clock-time the day is well used before a chill and ineffectual daylight takes hold.

These are the dark, short, nasty days. The "gathering gloom" seems just that—a close, heavy, stifling feel of rain and sodden air and clouds.

A few maple trees are still partly in leaf, however, and in the dim grayness their leaves shine as yellow as remembered sunlight.

November 11

Approaching winter imposes an armistice between man and nature.

Man is forced to retreat. He has farmed and brought in the harvest. He has hunted, and killed, and now puts away his gun. He has camped, and swum in the mountain lake; now the woods are snow-bound and the high lake is frozen over.

Man's dominion is at a halt. Winter takes over where man pulls back, and imposes its own discipline of cold and diminished daylight. Animals sleep, or scrounge for survival where they can—for this time, at least, safe from bullets and dependent on their own skills to outlast the winter.

The ground freezes and the dormant root and seed and bulb obey solely the laws of temperature and light.

A harshness, but a fairness to nature. All the life of the earth takes its chances on the spinning wheel now; man intervenes little in the wilderness, himself forced back by the season.

Despite glass-bubbled shopping centers and fog machines and oil furnaces, man must for a while adapt, restrict his movements, must temper his ambitions.

Man's dominion is at a temporary truce.

November 12

The cool days of late autumn are the perfect times to visit the beach. When bird and animal life is retreating from woods and fields, and human visitors depart the seashore, the beaches and tide pools continue to teem and surge with life. These are the original settlers, less affected by the push and pull of the seasons, therefore, simpler, less migrant and changeable; the life of the shore is one of uninvolved, rudimentary permanence. Here, the distinction between plant and animal life is not as clear, the beginnings of life seem arrested at the place of birth, and the struggle for survival operates at its lowest, most witless level, dependent on the advance and retreat of the tides, rather than the turn of the sun and its captive earth.

The lines are dim here. Rocks give shelter to a variety of forms, many of which are as vague and ill-defined (even in their own perfect symmetry) as organisms not yet embarked on any firm path of evolution. Startling shapes and macabre colors: the perfect convolution of the shell, as finely crafted as bowls; the purples and iridescent greens of sinister-looking perpetually damp plants; the scuttling bony sandflies; the crab eternally confined in its helmet. Varied and vulnerable to each other; such life forms seem alien in their sea-life styles.

People have collected the leaved, bulblike branches of the hydroid Obelia, believing they were taking home plants; actually these are colonies of animals organized into categories of labor and service like colonies of ants. The tentacles of one group indicate these are the ones that gather food for the entire community; the others, long and tubelike with no mouth parts, are given over entirely to reproduction.

Amid the seaweed, brown and glistening-bulbed on the rocks, the slim *Caprella*, an animal that looks much like another branch of seaweed, swaying in the water, in its color and form no more than a brown thready filament.

The starfish, brilliantly orange and strikingly shaped, is confined in its rigid case of spine, seemingly barely able to move, and yet can pry open a clam or oyster with comparative ease. It mounts the resistant shellfish in a curious drawn-up posture, like the motions of seduction, and applying selective pressure, pulls with its ingenious tube feet.

Sea anemones, brightly beautiful as decadent flowers, vivid in red and pink and orange, or ethereal emerald, are innocent-looking with their tentacles extended and open, and are lethal in their behavior; the reaching tentacles trap and sting small creatures coming within that net.

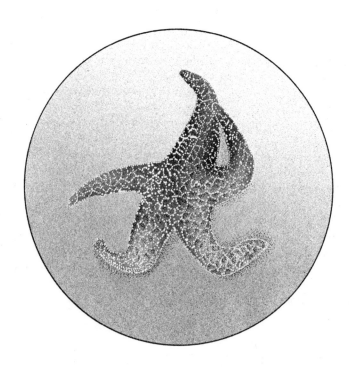

On the sands and in tide pools, life forms are more readily apparent as creatures—far down the scale, if evolution is considered to be a line of vertical ascent, but more accessible of recognition as possessing that indefinable quality of life misnamed awareness. The periwinkle, striped and shaped like water-formed rock, is perhaps taking the first steps toward earth life; many of these have been found outside of water, and surviving quite as well.

These are the laboratories of life, the empty oceans that are in fact crowded to bursting with life, the continuing experiments of nature. Here, the patterns merge: agates like eyes catch the light and wink, shells like seeds lie strewn on the beach. What is rock and what is animal and what is plant are not obvious or easy to name, and the barren rocks hammered at by the leap and retreat of waves have a desolate look under the ragged clouds of a November sky. Man, who had his beginnings in water, feels more affinity with the roaming seagull, to the wind-hoarse cry which indicates a creature with a brain, simple as that brain may be. The gull may not be entirely free, certainly not; on the other hand, lonely, but equipped with wings and voice, he expresses the mood of the ocean to man's ears, and seems both free, and aware of the penalties of that freedom. His is the voice that speaks to the human walking on the edge of the shore.

November 13

Madrona trees have an untidy disheveled air in November, as great strips of bark peel and fall to the ground. All year the great trees have dropped blossoms, berries, then shed their leaves (immense heaps of hard, waxy leaves pile at their trunks in August like middens), and now the trees have a totally coming-apart look. The bark is reddish, and lies in thin curling scraps on the ground like scrolls.

This is a perplexing tree—evergreen, yet always shedding some leaves. *Arbutus menziesii* is a hardwood, but the wood, heavy with moisture, is virtually useless; it does not even burn well in a fireplace. The trees are immense, yet have a deceptive foreshortened look of tangled low branches.

The Pacific madrona lives near salt water, along the coast and often at the exact edge of the sea, with outreaching curled arms twisted into wind patterns.

Ragged, slovenly, but it has the look of an ancient prototype of a tree, and in salt spray and fog, the red bark is a warm and cheering color.

November 14

FENCES

Birds build fences in their minds. The territorial instinct to divide and claim and protect property is strong, but can be self-defeating: the bird often restricts himself totally to just that piece of land and sky he has claimed. If anything happens—cutting of trees, felling of a power pole—the bird is helpless and disoriented, a dispossessed tenant with no property rights. The boundaries have been so carefully measured that if they are changed, the bird flies erratically and confused, seeking for the familiar. Free as a bird! He will fly to the edges of the invisible boundary and suddenly turn back, as if he had crashed into a pane of glass. The wall still exists in his mind.

Passionate residents, such birds will helplessly remain committed to one piece of destroyed property, rather than take the risk of intruding on another bird's territory—a territory held by the barrier of song.

Men, on the other hand, build fences to set off their land, to stake the claim. Fences, wood or wire, lead to quarrels between neighbors, winter repairs, painting and mending. Fences are easily knocked down, by November storm, by snow, by roaming cattle, or the great trespasser—wind.

November 15

Winter seems a masculine thing. The seasons have their physical attributes of coloring and moods, and November introduces the cold drive of aggression and change.

Spring and summer were totally feminine, with their ornaments of leaves and flowers—now, bare brown trees, storm-heaped rocks; the engineers are at work rebuilding. Mother Nature has been replaced by a bitter chauvinistic bachelor. Few matings now, or nest-building, only the storm-squalls of powerful and aggressive Scorpio.

A few redwings will winter along the eastern coast. These will all be males.

November 17

Benjamin Franklin disliked the idea of having the bald eagle as the national bird—the bird was a bad image for the young country, being a slovenly builder and obviously a robber. He has the unlikable habit of pursuing another bird, an osprey, for example, until that bird drops its prey, and then snatching it away from him. The turkey was nominated. (Previously someone had suggested the phoenix.) The eagle won out, and on June 20, 1782, the bird was elected to his post as a national emblem.

Today, the bird is much scarcer than it was, and a cousin, the golden eagle, is a threatened species. Even national symbols are not safe; the handsome large bird is an attractive trophy.

Big in size and in its habits, the eagle builds nests in cliffs or high trees that are mended and remodeled annually. Over the years (one nest was reported used for thirty-five years) the house becomes an impressive size and height: six feet tall and six feet across.

Fond of fish, the eagle haunts lakes, rivers and beaches, willing to steal or to hunt for food. The bird roams the great canyons of the hills to capture lizards and mice, anything small and moving that strikes its fancy. It will threaten other birds with its great beak and talons—an aggressive, overbearing display of pomp and power. Still, its rapaciousness is overemphasized; despite legends, it does not carry away children.

At maturity, the bird is unmistakably "bald," with white head and white tail; until then he is a mottled dark brown, occasionally mistaken for the golden eagle.

On a gray November day, against a cloud-filled backdrop, the eagle suggests that look of majesty and domination which early Americans conceived their rightful image to be.

Wings outspread—a mighty seven-foot span—he seems master of the air and harsh crag. He drops to a cliff ledge and stands, head slightly turned, eyes surly, beak downturned; he looks as if he both remembers past grudges and is quick to take offense again. The airs of immense age and anger and pride are his.

November 19

These are the days of primal hungers, of cravings for the foods of the earth. A root instinct gives a desire, not for meat alone, but for simple homely things: squash, pumpkins, thick soups, roasted chestnuts, plain bread with a solid feel to it, baked beans, gingerbread— the root things.

Celebrate November by baking acorn bread:

1 c acorn meal	4 T sugar
1 c flour	1 lg egg, beaten
3 t baking powder	1 c milk
1 t salt	3 T salad oil
⅓ c nutmeats, chopped	

Sift together dry ingredients, make a well, and add liquids. Mix just enough to moisten. Bake in a greased loaf pan 30 minutes at 400 degrees.

November 20

A November day is often wrapped in fog like a cocoon.

At the coast, the fog, silver-gray, chill and damp, seems a living, active thing, moving inland and rising up the hills, the breath of the ocean itself. Fog swirls and interrupts the pattern of rocky cliffs and trees. Shapes appear and reappear, fade to dim indistinctness, emerge again like dark pencil strokes of tree or rock. The sea itself is lost and hidden behind the fog.

In the valleys, fog is slow and heavy, hanging low, often so dense that at midday cars creep with their lights on; the fog seems an immense immovable weight. Fog fills out the empty spaces, obliterates shape and form. Sounds are muffled. Planes do not travel. Lights burn all day in obscure buildings. Distances are tricky things to guess. A city is a ghost town in its pallid shroud.

Storms of wind and rain, or blizzards, wreak havoc in lively fashion—tearing, plunging, raking. Even lightning, gaudy as a beacon gone wild, stabs and destroys.

Only a heavy fog, without palpable substance or sound or movement, simply by standing still, can so effectively hinder man's activities. At its thickest, heaviest worst, it brings everything to full stop.

November 21

Storms seem violent and rude interruptions to the measured march of nature, but what is called destruction is rearrangement of a sort, even revitalization. After wind and rain, a parenthesis, a quiet hollow of time and an open space: (   ).

The unscheduled times of nature are opportunities to see the bounty of the storm. Rain and high winds have brought to the forest the sparkle of trees and moss, spilled glinting leaves; the litter of the camper and visitor has been washed away, and the woods have a grand primeval look once more. New mushrooms have sprung up on log and brush. On the beach, the storm has brought in agates, shells, tiny indeterminate rocks, iridescent or gray-green, sometimes polished to tiny perfect discs. Along the Pacific Northwest beaches a blue-green float or two from Japan will bounce, loosely attached to a rope of seaweed. In farm fields, proof of disturbed earth when rains wash to the surface old artifacts: an arrowhead, a blackened bowl. Moisture of rain, pressed and driven by the wind, diverts the stream, moves rock, rebuilds the soil.

November 22

THE GREAT SILENCE

The earth is quieter and gentler now in November. Fewer insects, fewer birds, people are in their houses. Winter is a retreat. In the countryside, a stillness of clearer air. Summer was noisy, with its chorus of birdsong, twitter, trill; drone and hum of insects, but now sounds are few and scarce: leaf fall, no more than whisper. A crow, raspily asserting his rights over disputed territory, rattle of scraping branches. Each small sound comes sharply distinct, from brittle rusty trees and frost-crisp ground. The time of muffled winter is at hand and nature prepares for the great silence. On a dark gray November day, when the sun is hidden, all of nature seems hushed and attentive, bound in a waiting silence. November is the time of purification.

November 23

In November the starling is a mottled or speckled brown-black, wearing his winter coat. Life is more serious in the winter; this is no time for the gaudy iridescence of the spring mating season.

Unloved and unwanted, the starling continues to fill the country. His most objectionable fault: there are simply too many starlings.

In 1890 and 1891 the birds—one hundred of them—were imported from Europe and released over Central Park. Since that time the tribe has grown into the millions, and for his resilience and adaptability the bird has brought upon his head dislike, taunts, and bullets.

They are accused of being noisy. The starling is a charming singer, ingeniously imitating other bird songs or developing his own melodies and whistles. They are called dirty. Their nests are said to be slovenly. (The starlings will nest anywhere convenient, even in a building cornice.) They drive away other birds—blackbirds, woodpeckers, flickers—and become doubly unpopular. They eat cherries off trees, and irate growers brandish rifles.

Hardy and adaptable, starlings are diligent in the business of survival. For all their aimless, zigzag manner of walking, and nondescript habits, they are proof of success. Determined and tough, the starling not only survives but multiplies and replenishes.

For this, he gets the nomination of being the least-loved bird.

November 24

A hawk's life seems an easy one. The job description reads: circle the sky, scan the earth, roam and explore the wind. Requirements: perfect eyesight, steel nerves, infinite patience.

Part of the job is the excitement of finding food, which day after day after day is the continual grinding necessity of a hawk's adventurous life. In November, the job is harder, and the hawk works with unflagging skill and commitment, sometimes moving south a ways in his search.

A red-tailed hawk will perch on the branches of a dead tree to study the possibilities: a roaming mouse or gopher or grasshopper or lizard; an enterprising redtail will even take on a rabbit. In falconry jargon, a hawk "stoops"—odd choice of word for the darting plunge. A hawk stoops to conquer.

The job has its dangers. The hawk may on occasion kill a chicken. Whether or not he does, he has incurred the ill will of farmers who shoot to kill any and every hawk—a mistake, for the hawk is doing a friendly service in dispatching insects and rodents. Still, when predator meets predator, the farmer wins; the hawk, soaring with the identifying red tail visible, is the loser. Searching for the target prey, he is himself too much a target.

Winter is his; he is too audacious to give up his space of sky, but there is no vacation. Like the policeman of the sky that he is, he is much maligned, and flies under penalty of death—a lot that is not particularly a happy one. But the glide and wheel of a hawk in a dour November sky seem a pure, essential statement of being.

November 26

Early settlers coming from England brought turkeys to the new country, only to discover the turkey was already here; despite its name, this is a native bird.

Big, flamboyant, this is an impressive bird in its wild state, a handsome flash of color in empty fields and brushland.

Presumably, the Pilgrims ate the bird, and thus started a tradition. Despite its size and plumage, the bird lacked charisma; it lost out to the bald eagle in the choice for national bird and has become domesticated and commonplace, destined to be the true national choice: a supermarket package of plastic and lifeless flesh.

November 27

Clouds rising to the zenith—inactivity! The Superior Man will pass this time in feasting and enjoyment.

–*I Ching*

November 28

The first snowfall, after gathering gray days, is still unexpected, always a surprise.

There is something astonishing and unpredictable in the first flakes drifting idly down, then falling in concentrated white flurries. The surprise is in the forgotten warmth and gentleness of snow; the air seems stilled and mild with the first flakes. A particular intensity to the light now, reflected upwards as the ground is covered.

The first snow coming in November may not last, but winter touches, lays a crystalline structure, the sky and earth merge in a translucent light. Trees and hills and brush stand captive in a white museum of frosted glass.

December 1

Patterns of December: Snowflakes. The folds and pleats of timelessly repeated hills. Lace of snow and delicate frost on plants.

December 2

These are the short, pallid days of winter. Clouds heavy and slow as snails move in a glasslike sky. Not much of a light span now; people rise and move about in the dark and go to work, and come back in the dark. The days have cold blue edges as late afternoon dissolves quickly into dusk. The shortness of the days, the cold insubstantial air and the ice-frosted trees all combine to give the earth a look of fragility. Earth and its life are at their most vulnerable now. The short brittle days are seeds against the coming year.

December 5

A snow cave is usually an emergency measure, a retreat in a storm, or a desperate hideaway when the route is lost and winter night comes early. Yet, a snow cave can be a peaceful place when winds would batter and rip a tent, and for a man of the right temperament it can be no squalid bivouac but a setting of dignity and serenity in which to smoke a pipe and watch the passing of the storm.

Like repairing a severed artery, the process of building a snow cave is best accomplished if the builder does not hurry. Four men, working in smooth team effort, can build a cave in an hour, if conditions are good. A lightweight blade of sheet aluminum alloy, slipped over an ice-axe shaft, is a good tool.

Needed: calm, deliberate effort, and fairly firm snow, at least six feet deep, and a side hill of snowdrift or streambank. Dig a hole in the snow, approximately three by four feet, and three feet deep. Remove snow on a drop sheet or tarp. From this hole, dig horizontally into the bank, three feet or more; this will be the entrance hall, with a tarp draped over the door. The main body of the cave will be widened and deepened to accommodate party members. The floor will be higher than the entry tunnel, trapping warm air and also letting any snowmelt run downhill. Poke a small ventilation hole through the roof with ski pole or ice axe.

A well and patiently built snow cave, with a smooth domed roof, will be surprisingly warm, or at least not uncomfortable, warmed by body heat and a candle or stove. A snow cave will not last—after two days its structure will have thawed downslope, but in the meantime it is a snug and serviceable burrow, and a good place from which to contemplate vistas of the most striking and purest beauty—the mountains at their most serene.

December 6

From the air the roofs of Yosemite, banking the narrow submerged valley, catch the light, look buoyant, granite that floats. The shape of Half Dome, rising at the head of the valley, is unmistakable, an arresting sculpture of broad bare top and one perfectly straight side as if the great dome had been smoothly sheared in two. Like the Matterhorn in Switzerland, Half Dome is so precisely itself, such a perfect recognizable shape of a mountain, that it seems living, and a conscious force or creation in itself. Light catches the granite, and the mountain beams, reflecting friendliness and intelligence.

On the trail and ladder route, Half Dome is no great climbing achievement up its forty-degree backside, without the cables and rungs a stiff Class IV; individuals have climbed the unrelenting face itself.

At first, Half Dome seemed hardly climbable. Professor Whitney announced solemnly that it was "perfectly inaccessible." "It never will be trodden by human foot." Later he retracted to the extent of adding a guarded "perhaps." John Conway attempted the climb, sending up a crew of small boys with rope, but found the smooth upper rocks impracticable—only for real lizards. Another valley resident, George C. Anderson, literally forged a way to the top. He drilled holes for eyebolts five or six feet apart, fastening his climbing rope to the bolts as he climbed, and accomplished this engineering feat in a few days.

Shortly after, John Muir himself made the climb, after the first winter storm. Despite fresh snow and slippery rock, Muir, with characteristic understatement, wrote that his climb was "without the slightest difficulty." He commented on the view, but also the minute homely things on the mountain: varieties of sedges and grasses, species of pine.

The trail is long to the summit; the climber passes through sweet-smelling pines, shadowy curves of trails, sees evidence of bears, and pines driven and shaped by the wind. The top of Half Dome, wind- and storm-bared, looks totally barren and is home to lizards and squirrels.

In the winter, a moon wanders near the crest of the Dome; snow edges the gentler slope, and the high wall of the mountain is darkly outlined. In a *trompe l'oeil* trick of angles and plane, the great thing of stone has a look of fragility, as if it were created only of light and shadow.

December 7

A winter storm on a beach is a fine and impressive thing to see—from a distance. The waves, high-stepping, advance and retreat, the water is the color of steel, and the breakers gleam, flung like spears at the rocky cliffs. A heavy driving rain obscures the horizon and there is only the rush and backward fall of the sea; the steady high roar of wind and waves is itself a silence. Logs are tossed about like twigs. The sea is in a rage, a steady beating advance and fury; and the arc of beach looks as if it will crumble and collapse before the assault. No human, no bird, in sight. Only the sea and the land, locked in their screaming embrace.

December 9

In December the first birds come to nest in the great rookeries of Everglades National Park. The "flintheads"—wood ibises—soar in the thousands above the labyrinth of islands in East River Rookery, their black-bordered white wings flashing. Soon will come the snowy egrets, the Louisiana herons, and the common egrets. In this subtropical national park, dedicated by President Truman in 1947, a display of plumage and flight, of eager jostling and pushing and clattering of vast varieties of scarce and exotic birds—appropriate in this setting of sepia waters and marshes and dusky mangrove canopies. Morning mists dissolve to a clear midday sun; the Everglades retain their look of primitive and essential youth—a warm and murky birthplace for nature's wild infants. The flat lands of the Everglades—geologically young—cling close to the sea; alligators and crocodiles share the waters here with birds searching for fish.

December 10

A SHORT HISTORY OF PAIN

How long is enough? Man has been on the earth a relatively short time—an eye-blink in the impassive gaze of creation—and already he is an endangered species, in spite of and partly because of his vast numbers. There is, possibly, too much man for earth; there is only so much oil, so much water, so many trees, all the things man is in need of, and he has underestimated his own capacity for survival. Writers like Isaac Asimov predict planetary homes in space as escape valves for a burgeoning population. Mars may yet be green, the canals filled, and a dreary moon mined for rocks and gravel to build freeways. Technology moves fast, but man moves slower, still emotionally an ape, swinging on the vines and reluctant to leave (altogether) his trees and his cave.

With his opposable thumb and his largely unused brain, man may or may not be long-lived; he is a newcomer with ambitions, and at one time the dinosaurs thought they owned the earth.

Man has a long and impressive record for his short stay: executions, tortures, wars, slavery, urban ghettos, punishment of women, religious wars, the stake, the rack, hatred and fear of the aging, Ku Klux crosses, Watergate, Kent State, Dachau, bonfires of witches, the McCarthy investigations, lynchings, the hands of thieves chopped off, assassinations, women forbidden to act as priests, babies left stuffed in garbage cans, welfare "for the lazy," the cross of Christianity, the rape of the land. Still, man goes on repeating himself, and this is his strongest instinct; abortions themselves are testimonies to the cruel reproductive instinct.

Some observers have seen a playful game in evolution, a sleight-of-hand trickery—now you see it, now you don't—of saber-tooth tiger or carrier pigeon. Actually, there is a profound inertia or resistance in evolution which tends to produce ultimately a mass-stamped standardized product; men destroy the mutant, the different, in a hundred available ways. Babies are survivors if they reach for the middle (children of extremely intelligent parents are slightly less intelligent; the middle ground is the safest place to be). T. S. Eliot's picture of the crab shuffle in the wasteland is a dim and solitary anguish, the fabricated God who will disappear when man dies.

The kingdom of the beasts is a singularly loveless hierarchy, and man its cruelest ruler, acting much of the time in fear. Far from being different from other animals, man is certainly a predator, at the apex of the food chain; man is more clever than intelligent, and his spineless cleverness may be his own undoing. It takes bravery to be an animal that thinks.

For some men a sense of rightness in the process of sharing, like the flower whose business is being a flower, knowing a link to this amazing life, feeling it is good to be an animal among animals on earth. Butterfly and edelweiss hunters lead short precarious lives of excitement, and seem not to be trying always to capture a particular species, but the form or essence of nature itself.

Many other men insist that there is something special about man that will ensure his immortality. Yet, to a coyote's eye, the coyote is the center of the universe.

December 11

Nature has perdurability. There is a lastingness to nature, even when abused, destroyed, altered; nature—or life—is a fluid, boundaryless thing that resists the cycles, the deaths and the new beginnings, the trial and error process; it can be pushed away, pinned back, but it keeps flowing over the edges again.

The redwoods reach up through the fog, as they have through the years. Land, neglected, becomes impenetrable wilderness once more; nature never neglects, but is the seeking, grasping opportunist. Stones have staying power; mountains are born and die but the rocks remain, and stone artifacts thousands of years old arise in the brooding hills of Calico, California, exposed under the archaeologist's pick, and delight and confound. In the alkali soil, all trace of man is gone, but the stones he worked on with his hands endure. The sea has an impassive face, continuous power at work, exposing new cliff faces, carving out rocky caves. The ocean endures.

Some forms of life have been so eminently successful that they linger unchanged; the turtle follows the ways of his ancestors. The sky is constantly changing, never the same from one day to the next, and remains the eternal sky.

December 12

Some people act in competition not with each other, or on their jobs, but in competition with nature, as if the entire world were simply a kind of gymnasium or a test situation in which one has to be continually passing obstacles, moving through difficulties, straining against the odds. In these people, aggression is turned against their own environment, and they seem always to be reaching for high scores, fighting to win the eye of an invisible referee.

One couple shared the hobby of mountain climbing. Both became strong, durable and adept climbers, leading mountaineering groups and other parties. Their one child learned as an infant that it would be left at home every weekend with a succession of babysitters. The man could carry heavier packs—impressive 80-90-pound loads—but his wife, gifted with an easy, natural balance, had a better time of it cramponing her way up steep ice slopes. Climbs became more difficult and dangerous. In the winter, the couple entered ski races. Even when the wife broke her ankle, there was only a temporary stop to this fevered activity. Some of their mountaineering expeditions took them into Canada and here their eyes were challenged by virgin peaks of great height and stern rock. Soon they were taking every vacation north.

They became strong and lean, with confident sunburned faces, and at home, in their comfortable suburb, they moved restlessly about, seeming displaced and ill at ease on flat land where there was nothing to test their powers of endurance, or their lung power, or their ability to find their way up through the crevasse and boulder maze of a mountain. Now there was no talk of scenery or pretty campsites or leisurely walks on a forest trail. They made their friends vaguely uneasy: how high was a particular mountain? Had it been climbed before? Other climbers were put off by the intensity of this single-minded drive. Why did everything have to be done the hard way?

When it rained, the couple still climbed, or at least made the attempt, and then began to compete in mountain marathon races, simply running up and down foothills in mass competition. No prize was enough. Both were highly intelligent people, possessed of great determination, but now they began to neglect their jobs, and talked little to each other; what was there to say if there was not a mountain immediately to be climbed, gear to be packed for a long, punishing expedition?

One day the couple divorced. Their friends were surprised ("they had so much in common!"). The man still climbs, impossible, frightening routes; because he is older and his reactions slowed, he has had a couple of minor accidents. His wife still runs on the mountainsides, up and down, up and down, even when there is no mass race; she has become thin and brown and looks older than she is. Nothing can be hard enough, or lonely enough, when nature is neither friend nor enemy but a silent and waiting opponent.

December 14

On a winter evening, in many a Midwest farmhouse, the wishbook was an institution and entertainment. The bulky Sears catalog was brought out to the round oak table, and all the family looked through its pages. These were stories for adults—with pictures—almost as exciting as the new radio on its own table, that didn't always work too well, despite its howl arrester. These were collections of tantalizingly pictured delights for youngsters. With Christmas approaching, it wasn't too soon to ask for a goat harness, or a wagon, or the Flirty Flossy doll ("with eyes that wink, blink, and flirt"). There was never much money to spend; when decisions were finally made (but even the delays and the deliberations were agonizingly sweet and confusing), Dad would fill out the order form, using a carefully sharpened pencil, and attending with solemnity to the task, as befitted such an important event.

In the meantime, there were all those dazzling things to consider: Dr. Wine's Health Corset for mother (supports the abdomen and internal organs); an array of diamond rings, each with a girl's name—Clarice, Annette, Marguerite—larger on the page than they could ever look in real life. Mother could imagine them twinkling in their settings of white or green gold filigree, but she could not for the life of her imagine one of them *on her finger*. Dad's eye fell again on the new Hercules Boiler, and the improved feed mix, and Dr. Edward's bag balm. Thinking of Christmas just ahead, they looked at the stockings for boys and girls, each filled with 25 toys at $1.98 (compare with others regularly selling for $2.50 and $2.98).

Most of the things in the book were useful. If prosperity burgeoned across America and a depression seemed unthinkable, it was still true that the house had chilly corners, particularly on a winter night, when the cold wind seemed waiting to seize the house in its teeth and shake it, and one of the cows looked sick with a dim brooding expression in her eye, and there was that nuisance of the outdoor privy—if only they could install the new Handee Indoor Toilet ("guaranteed to save the embarrassment of public gaze"). Not that there was much public out here to gaze at anyone, out here in the wind-scarred, snow-lumped fields. Wool stockings, and union suits at $.68, took up part of the order forms; union suits that would freeze on the outdoor line and be brought in like stiff cutouts that could be stood against a wall, frozen scarecrow arms suspended.

Rural America was hopeful, but the man and woman knew their roles, and their respective duties; it would never have occurred to either one that a man was not the head of the house, support and authority, and for the woman: that sweet steamy world of cooking, cleaning, and laundry. Sometimes she wore overalls, going out to the barn, when the wind tossed and pulled, and her hair was early unabashedly gray, but in the pages of the wishbook she saw herself as feminine and cherished, a creature to wear a box-pleated dress (all silk crepe, $10.98) and use Marvella Powder ($.42) in a modern vanity case.

America lived confident in the magic spell of expectancy. Modern society has lost not so much its old values (whatever they were, for instincts and drives remain the same) but something of hope, or trustfulness. Now, even the newest catalog seems already faintly soiled and archaic; a wispy nostalgia exists in its array of ephemeral and disposable artifacts. People have become dry-mouthed in a time of layoffs and job competition and swollen prices and the casual easy corruption of politicians and corporations. They have lost a sense of expectancy.

December 15

The beaver has been admired for his industry, and certainly he is a good steady worker, not taking time to hibernate, but in December still acting as engineer and dam builder. Indians predicted the severity of winter weather on the amount of food supply the beavers would lay in at the beginning of the season.

The animal has a striking ability to adapt the environment to his own needs. With long, furiously growing, orange incisors that must be kept short by constant gnawing, he fells aspen or willow or other water-loving trees, gnaws the logs to easily carved lengths, and floats or drags the food to his cache. Sheltered in his retreat of sticks plastered with mud, which may be eight feet high and sixteen feet across, he leaves the lodge (always it has an underwater entrance) to look for food, a branch or twig, and breathes air bubbles trapped under the ice of a frozen pond. Excellently built for his aquatic engineering career, he possesses a remarkable quantity of fat; webbed hind feet; a flat tail that is rudder and paddle, and slaps the water firmly to sound an alarm; and a handsome fur coat waterproofed by oil glands and shielded by long guard hairs. Largest of the North American rodents, the beaver may be three to four feet long and weigh up to an impressive seventy pounds.

People have noted the animal's intelligence; groups of beavers give and take assistance in constructing lodges and dams. Cooperative, sometimes playful, the beaver is a friendly and feisty youth, much engaged in companionable wrestling, and can be trained to come to visitors at winter ponds for food. Perky-faced, with an endearing look of alertness, the beaver has even been a sometime house guest, but will eat away the legs of tables or chairs if not stopped.

In winter, his handsome chestnut fur is at prime, the fur that almost led to his extinction when trappers sought it for hats. The beaver's coat has also been used for currency, and when the state of Oregon was young and gold plentiful, the Oregon Exchange Company coined $5 and $10 gold pieces—each coin stamped with a beaver—containing 8 percent gold, more than that in U.S. Mint coins. The gold pieces disappeared when U.S. currency became plentiful, and only a few exist now as mementoes of that time of enterprise and abundance.

Castor canadensis has at times been too industrious for his own good; he will dam an irrigation ditch just as he would a stream, and is capable of felling a number of fruit trees in a single night of work. For this diligence, he wins the hostility of farmers. Beaver lifts have therefore transported beavers into mountainous country, where they can build dams which will serve conservation by checking erosion. The animals have been crated and dropped by parachute in Idaho forests; the adaptable beavers have promptly set to work in their new homes.

Green bark is the beaver's favorite food, and he is a selective gourmet if the area is good. Primarily nocturnal, he must be on the watch for bear or wolverine, often using smoothly constructed logging trails for escape routes. Under water he is a skillful swimmer with large-capacity lungs.

Occasionally, a prosperous beaver will weigh as much as a hundred pounds, a handsome furred Paul Bunyan of the forest world.

December 16

ACROBAT WITH A TEMPER

In the summer, he led an easy life, up in the mountains, in the company of a few other males. Majestic in a poised stance on the rocks, he was a wary acrobat, ready to disappear if alarmed—bounding away on the cliffs.

Now in December he has mating on his mind. The great bighorn bucks meet—poised like duelists forty feet apart—and then rush to collide in a battering, crashing, head-on charge of the curling horns. The impact echoes a mile away. Time after time the great heads meet, rock dazedly; horns splinter, blood flies. After an hour or so one is victor. For him, the harem.

Mating is a short, passionate, and violent event. Afterwards the male loses interest, and the young lamb is the ewe's total responsibility.

Winter is also a time of hardship for the bighorn. His alpine grasses are buried under snow, and he must drop to lower mountain levels, always risking attack by wolves and cougars.

Still, he endures. He has escaped extinction, though the curling horns are a prize trophy (growth rings denote age). Stricter hunting controls help. He survives the winters, occasionally saved by air drops of food in certain areas. He survives parasites and ticks and blowflies and disease.

A spectacular animal, given to spectacular displays of dominance and courage, coolly at ease on formidable mountain rocks, in the harsh desert, the bighorn sheep endures.

December 17

The attitude of many conservationists seems brutal, a peculiarly harsh idealism, and in the end, inhuman. To the human mind, the value of a thing is tested by its usefulness, its purpose, and of what value is an unseen world? Why should the last meager portions of wilderness be saved, inaccessible to most, if not all? Little utility to dense brush and woodland of the North Cascades, or hidden unapproachable lakes that can be visited only by animals and birds who themselves exist without demonstrable purpose. A few condors—stragglers—in California; these things have little to do with reality, with the miserable business of building houses and finding water supply and getting jobs and making a living. These lonely wilderness areas and remote animals stand outside the immediate reality and necessity of human existence, and are therefore foolishly impractical.

The oil companies plumb the coastline, and a few protest, but obviously their outcries are foolish; their reaction is against the now, the enjoyment and use of the now, and progress is inevitably linked to destruction of the environment.

Actually the unseen world is a retreat to which the mind can escape; man has no need of UFO's or communication from lost universes. If all the wilderness and its shy things are gone, there is no retreat left, only concrete buildings and the narrow, threatened personal spaces of each individual. The quality of wilderness is its mystery and inaccessibility—its uselessness that suggests to the mind the infinite possibilities of the universe. When all the wilderness is consumed, man has no place left to turn, nothing on which to whet his imagination and his desires, and his mind itself will shrivel, become dry and trapped. The human soul has need of green.

To the conservatives, concerned with profits and annual reports, conservationists are the most radical of visionaries. To save wild beauty, parts of which may never be seen by anyone, and to fight with a passionate conviction, is a denial of all rational instinct. The conservationists possess a vision.

December 18

This is the harsh testing time for animals. For each, a particular method to live out the winter: hibernation, or dormancy (the shallow hibernators), or ingenious adaptation, or a single-willed dedication to survival that takes precedence over all other instincts. (Men in survival situations, even passively waiting for rescue, have no time for sex.)

Some adaptations have evolved over the years. The hare grows long stiff hairs along the edges of his feet which give him better purchase on the snow. The grouse grows a kind of natural crampons on his toes, sharp traction points.

Overwintering birds take their chances. Deer beat out well-defined grounds and paths, protecting and making accessible their diminished food supply. The coyote gets what it can; from the stomachs of hardy, try-anything-once coyotes have been fished such odd items as flashlight batteries and cans and cardboard. The condor, his heavy neck feathers bunched up like a muffler against the cold, sits arrested through the spasm of the storm.

Winter is a time of energies expended with virtually no replacement; photosynthesis is greatly reduced or nonexistent; animals find snow travel strenuous, food caches buried.

Survival of the fittest is a possibility; death by starvation and exposure occur also to the fit. God's eye is busy watching the sparrows fall.

December 19

On a clear winter day, walk in the country and see the record of other excursions:

December 20

The towns are full of Christmas trees. At one time, when the forests were so generously full that it seemed they would go on forever, people brought home immense, ceiling-touching trees, to be hidden under radiant spangled adornment, standing like brides behind closed doors. Commercial growing of Christmas trees has become a profitable business (hundred-acre farms near Puyallup, Washington are a minor but stable industry) and it seems less sad, or anachronistic, to bring in a truckload of trees grown especially for the occasion. Would Christmas be Christmas without a real tree? Few people want or can afford to buy a living tree of any size to be planted outside, and plastic trees have a kind of joyless rigidity associated with discount stores and plastic snowmen; it is a measure of a touching faith, or innocence of spirit, that most Americans still celebrate the holiday with a real tree, and some go into the woods—with a permit—to cut down a tree.

Some American Indians, seeking to soothe or distract a tree they were about to cut down, for the building of a totem pole or a canoe, used to approach the victim: "Oh, beautiful tree! How straight and well-made you are! How fitting that you now should become a straight and swift canoe!"

Christmas tree shoppers are more matter-of-fact and seek out a fat glossy young fir, all its holes and spaces plumped out, much as they look for a turkey. Balsam fir, Douglas fir, and the Norway spruce are all favorites; green and waxy, the appropriate bearers of lights and gifts in the hiatus of winter. As much as anything else, the moment of Christmas is in a tree's fragrance. In that sweet spicy scent of needles and green is this year's Christmas and all the seasons before.

December 21

The shortest day of the year, the lowest point of the earth's turn. Heavy low fogs muffle and blot out the coastline, and inland, winds and snow visit the valleys. Morning, and a chill reluctant daylight, seems hardly to have arrived before it is gone again. Even the stars of winter seem cold and far away and the moon cold white ashes. The sun reaches the limit of its journey south of the celestial equator moving on the Tropic of Capricorn. Tomorrow winter begins.

December 23

ORDEAL OF THE STARS

Many astronomers believe that the star of Bethlehem was a real star, one of the singularly bright stars that pass through the earth's atmosphere on their way to unguessed destinations, and reconstructed visualizations display that night of the unknown star's splendid travels.

The star becomes the symbol of the otherness, the message from the void. Where is the star of Bethlehem now? Perhaps racing still on some journey beyond imagination or belief. Or it may be that the mysterious light of the East is a collapsed star, now dead, and only a black aperture to other stars, other worlds.

December 24

The vigil of Christmas begins. This is the holy season, the great event and supreme holiday of the Western world, but at its base are the peculiarly human emotions and human will; what people worship is the affirmation of the self. The season is all the more poignant because it is an earthly human thing; far from being divine, it is the most profane. Human beings and their wishes and their prayers have a way of vanishing down through the centuries, and Christmas is a fleshly way of saying that humans exist, and will exist, and have needs and desires that are important, in a hard and implacable natural world. The great secret of Christmas is its recurrence of human hopes, the warm and sensual physical; the mystery is the personal awareness of man in an environment he did not create.

When winters were a time of testing, and death the penalty for relaxation of attention, the first winter celebrations were the pagan rebellions against the stark, down-to-earth, bare-stripped simplicity of winter. Human beings want light, and warmth, and the knowledge of other human hearts and bodies, and the seeking, vulnerable fact of life. Christmas is an intrusion into silence, an affirmation of human hopes and desires—a bottle with a message adrift in the sea.

The pictographs of departed Indians seem no more than the clawmarks of a bear on a tree, a signal to other bears who may pass by. In the cold impersonality of time, the family and the crèche are the stylized pinpoint of hope.

168

December 25

A man and his wife who went skiing every year during the winter holidays decided one year not to make the drive back to the city on Christmas Eve. Traffic was heavy and possibly dangerous on the snow-glistened highway; the couple thought without anticipation of cocktail parties and a heavy, tiresome dinner. In the late afternoon they strapped packs on their backs (down sleeping bags, freeze-dried foods, a light sturdy tent) and skied up a gentle trail, away from the lodge and ski runs. Silence that Christmas Eve, with the skiers gone, and no sounds from any highway; the couple were astonished into stillness themselves by the silence and blackness of the woods. Never had they been in so quiet a place. Only, now and then, the creak of a branch as snow dropped.

Talking little, they set up the tent in a space between trees on the knoll, and watched the gray sky slowly, imperceptibly darken. They ate their supper of soup and stew; as a gesture toward festivity, there was fruitcake and a little wine that the husband had put in his pack. They watched the hills disappear in the twilight; trees like firm exclamation points were underlined with dark shadow strokes on the drifted and compacted snow.

In the silence and darkness the animals were hidden, though there had been tracks near their narrow ski prints, and the wife remembered the legend that at midnight the animals would speak. But at midnight there was no way of testing the legend; they were themselves asleep, pleasantly tired, wrapped in silence and the warmth of their sleeping bags. Overhead, stars were suspended in an abyss of time.

In the morning they woke, suddenly, with first light. Soon the sun came, turning the snow rosy, and the morning glittered coldly. They fed crumbs of fruitcake to a small congregation of chattering birds that had arrived, and wished they could hold out their palms filled with mealworms. It was, they thought, the most beautiful morning they had ever seen, the trees and the hills themselves now filled with light and sound as snow melted off branches and the distant ridges sparkling like a child's thought of a world made of sugar, a ridged and unfolding world going on infinitely beyond eye's reach. When, later, they went down to their car and drove home, friends said, But weren't you lonely?

December 27

Snowflakes, in their perfect varied geometry, a generosity of forms, reflect the tendency in nature of things to come together, to crystallize, to form and repeat the patterns of infinity. Each snowflake is individual, perhaps, only because the human eye and mind can register only a portion of what exists, or can be imagined; the senses register a small fraction of the universe. Snowflakes represent a jigsaw puzzle, or the shift and juggle of the kaleidoscope. Some of the pieces are missing, and the unseen and invisible whole can only be speculated on.

December 29

Nature is circular. The planets, stars, the dome of sky, repeat the circular patterns of cells and life. All of life and creation dance in the circle of communal mortality, which is to say immortality, for in these coldly logical circles there is no beginning and therefore no end. Earth itself was a fragment of a greater circle, and the proteins that built life were stray fragments from other skies. God's real name may be the formula of an enzyme. In the precise-stepping ballet of snowflakes, the measured art of nature, which seems random only because the patterns are so large.

December 30

Nature is the expanding circle, the expanding cell. From the first cosmic awakening, the ever widening grasp. Life has an impact on the unknowing void.

The end of the year approaches, but there is no end yet. In each cell an ebb and flow operates, in the rhythm of the circle, and there is no running out. Death carries an hourglass, but nature operates on the leisurely move of the pendulum. The long slow pull of time and light, inhibition and promotion, now advancing, now retreating, governs every plant and every animal, in every round of the cycle.

December 31

A December day may be so brilliantly clear that one can see into the shaping center of the world, the uncoiling spring, into the earthworks.

Earth Magician shapes this world.
　Behold what he can do!
Round and smooth he molds it.
　Behold what he can do!
Earth Magician makes the mountains.
　Heed what he has to say!
He it is that makes the mesas.
　Heed what he has to say.

Earth Magician shapes this world;
Earth Magician makes its mountains;
Makes all larger, larger, larger.
Into the earth the Magician glances;
Into its mountains he may see.

—Pima Indian chant

Winter:
The Dark Time

January 1

Patterns of January: ice crystals, trees like empty racks, hills heaped with snow, these stately pleasure domes looking closer and larger under their white weight; snow blossoms bloom on tree branches. Patterns of leaf scars on the trees: a heel plate on the American elm, wedge on the horse chestnut, triangles on the red maple, heart-shaped on the Kentucky coffee tree.

January 4

THE SNOWSHOE EXPRESS

John Thompson was a blue-eyed Norwegian who had come to the United States as a boy, and at twenty-nine had gone through a dissatisfying career of gold panning and ranching in California. Hard-muscled, taciturn, he was a loner who kept looking for something, a challenge from life. In early January, 1856, he found it. The item was in a Sacramento newspaper:

People Lost to the World
Uncle Sam Needs a Mail Carrier
Placerville to Carson City

Thompson knew personally how slow the mails were; months late he had received the letter telling of his mother's death from influenza.

Major George Chorpenning had the government mail contract. One party took forty-seven days to get across the Sierras. Heavy storms stopped the mail altogether.

Twenty-nine-year-old Thompson pondered the newspaper item, and came up with a solution that was so ambitious and unlikely that it worked. Recalling his boyhood in Norway, he built snowshoes—clumsy-looking homemade skis that were ten feet long and weighed twenty-five pounds. On these heavy and awkward shoes John Thompson began a long and incredible career as mailman.

His first trip was over the Placerville-Johnson-Luther Pass route, between Placerville and Carson Valley—a distance of about ninety miles. Later he traveled the Big Trees route to Hope Valley, then down Carson Canyon to Genoa, Nevada. It took three days to make the journey, and two or three more to return.

These were the routes the first pioneers had taken, and later, the men hungry for gold. In winter these routes were treacherous under opaque skies and spitting storms. Thompson performed his duties in Viking style. Carrying an average of sixty pounds of mail on his back (the bag often included medicine, tools, and assay samples), he traveled without overcoat or blankets. Beef jerky and biscuits were his food. He carried no compass, simply took his bearings by lichen-covered rocks, and the stars.

During the day, exertion kept him warm; at night he built a campfire and slept on a bough bed. During blizzards, he holed up in snowcaves to wait out the storms. He was never injured, and lost only once, when he was temporarily struck with snowblindness. He became an epic figure—"Snowshoe Thompson."

For twenty years, Thompson lived on his California ranch near Carson Valley and carried the mail. His pay: many promissory notes, and a little cash.

On one trip, he found James Sisson lying alone, freezing to death in a remote cabin near Lake Valley. The luckless Sisson had been there twelve days, without fire for the last four, and had for food only a little flour left. His feet were frozen.

Snowshoe Thompson traveled all night to bring help, and then left again at once, snowshoeing to Sacramento for anaesthetic for the life-saving business of amputation.

Skiing was newly in vogue; Norwegian miners working in Plumas County challenged each other to ski races, achieving speed by using "dope," a kind of patent medicine, on the bottoms of the skis. Thompson, innocent of such measures, was badly outraced, but bet $100 that no one could follow him across the country without breaking his neck. He got no takers.

Major Chorpenning died bankrupt, and mail contracts were never formalized, but Thompson went on carrying the mails. It was a job to be done. He battled committee meetings in Washington, D.C. unsuccessfully; the postal service was entangled in bureaucratic red tape.

John Thompson died May 15, 1876 at his California ranch. He was buried in Genoa, Nevada, where on a marble tombstone, a pair of crossed skis are carved. "In memory of John A. Thomson [the Norwegian spelling]." At the end, Thompson had held $6,000 worth of promissory notes from California postmasters.

Now, a modern, well-engineered highway crosses the mountains and skiers romp in the winter. Sometimes, when the sky is heavy and lowering with an approaching storm, the mountains again look difficult and dangerous—a testing ground for Vikings and heroes.

January 6

The winter days are short, no more than fragments. A pallid and ineffectual sun pierces the fog and clouds, but lingers briefly and without warmth. At twilight, the moon is a chilly half-smile in the sky. These are the short empty spaces of time, snatched between periods of darkness, narrow and pinched with cold. January is a halting, feeble month, a time that gives a glimpse of a world without Brother Sun.

January 7

THE WOLF IS A GENTLEMAN

Two snowshoers slowly plodding up a snow-buried logging road glimpsed a figure standing along the road, in the midst of stumps and logs. The animal stood motionless, regarding their approach. The hiker in the lead made excited motions to his companion, who hurried gamely on the clumsy snowshoes to see.

Then the wolf, without a sound, turned unhurriedly and began to lope down the rocky bank of the hill. He stopped to look back, paused once or twice, and then vanished into the woods.

The two hikers grinned and shouted at each other. "We saw him!"

They were lucky. Few people see wolves; fewer yet get close enough to see that impassive look or the silent dignity of the timber wolf.

Viewed at close hand in the open, a wolf is an impressive animal. There is a look of calm intelligence to the face, an almost speaking expression of alert eyes and ears and slender muzzle. Resembling a little a large German shepherd dog, the wolf has no air of domesticity, but instead appears totally independent and unassailable, with the color of gray stone in his fur, and a sharpness to the raised nose. This is no friendly dog.

His fur and stance tell what his environment is like; most timber wolves are of a "lean and hungry look." His silence and watchful expression speak of a guarded caution in a hostile world.

Even in retreat, a wolf has dignity.

Two factors, high intelligence and mutual cooperation, keep the wolf alive when by all rights (supposed enemy of man, sometime enemy of sheep and cattle ranchers) he should have been dead long ago.

That he has been considered the most rapacious and cruel of animals, the evil destroyer of Red Riding Hood, and the cruel hunter of snow-crippled travelers, attests only to the myth-making qualities of the animal. Some primal longing in man makes that feral brother the glimmering werewolf, and the wolf becomes a somber metaphor in opposition to the human mind. The savage beast should have been extinct; he has been hunted, trapped, shot at from airplanes, despised and feared by unanimous vote. Ten years after the Pilgrims landed, they set a bounty on the wolf, and the pattern was set.

Still, Romulus and Remus were suckled by a friendly wolf. A Seattle writer, Helmuth, took a wolf in his home and found her a loving creature, enormously shy and possessed of quivering nerves. Lois Crisler raised young wolves and probed the splendid secrets both of their devotion, and their stubborn reserve, found music in their howling. These are animals that love to be free, that retain their dignity even in the soiled setting of a zoo, where they pace endlessly, refusing to give up their independence totally.

Once common over the United States, a scant hundred or so wolves roam today, mostly in the Rocky Mountains, in the woods of the Great Lakes region, and here and there in national parks. The animal lives a thoughtful, well-organized life. His family courtesy and decency are innate; the wolf is a gentleman.

He is regular in his habits, a fact which often leads to his downfall. A group of wolves will make a circuit of their runways—hunting routes, elliptical in shape, using game trails or dry washes or canyons—with determined regularity approximately every nine days, marking the scent posts. Thus he becomes a predictable prey for hunters.

The wolf is a family man. He mates for life. Loyal wolves have mourned beside a trapped mate; sometimes both have died together. Litters of six to twelve pups are born in the spring in rocky dens or hillside burrows; high fecundity but bitterly low survival.

The male both hunts for food, and stands guard; both parents eat and then produce the predigested food for the pups. On occasion, a friendly and helpful male takes an "uncle" stance; with avuncular generosity assisting in bringing up the young wolves. Soon the practice hunting trips begin.

Rarely does a wolf attack a man. The stories of mass attacks on humans in Europe have largely been disproved; rabies may have accounted for some instances of uncharacteristic ferocity.

Weighing up to 125 pounds and more, grizzled in color, the wolf has a stern beauty. This is a hard-muscled animal, built for heavy and demanding duty, graceful and courageous, with sharp senses and fast-running legs and slashing teeth. Hunting in packs, wolves display a keenness both of the senses and brain; each member of the silent pack performs his part in bringing down the prey of deer or rabbit—sometimes, even a moose. After a successful hunt, a wolf will gorge himself to stupor; there may be hungry days ahead.

His howl is tingling and inexplicable; this is the true call of the wild. He uses his thick plume tail much like a dog, wagging it in pleasure, or tucking it away in fright.

The two snowshoers may have felt a thrill in coming so near upon a wolf, and a vestigial sense of fable-nurtured fear or at least

caution mingled in their surprise, and an anticipation of discovery, but the free, wild wolf is cautious in his curiosity, restrained by his memories and his life of belonging to rocks and trees and the night shadows.

Nor does the wolf—persecuted, viciously hunted and slaughtered (the smell of man must be an ugly one to him)—exhibit a desire for retribution.

The wolf is a gentleman.

January 9

On farms in the Midwest, cold is an intense purposeful thing, a living, steady companion that must be reckoned with daily. As the temperature drops, the cold is a sober reality, imposing its unstopping discipline and demands.

People cannot now become careless. The horses and cows have to be watched; a sick cow in January is a sad liability. Food supplies are counted and checked; snowplows will not be able to fight heavy storms. Last year's harvest is eaten frugally. In a chill blue dusk, the house and buildings have a Gothic look of austerity and purpose; people living on the land have a sense that theirs is the real world, a world with meanings that city folk cannot know. Neighbors telephone each other; they see each other less frequently now in these days of heavy cold, but their voices reach out to each other.

The days march; there is little wind and no storm comes, but the cold is there, intense and solid, just outside the door. In the upstairs of old farmhouses, children sleep with their feet curled against hot bricks wrapped in newspapers, and their breath emerges in little steamy vapors from a hole in the covers. Going to school is a major expedition; a fragile body is wrapped for protection in layers of clothes and muffler and scarves and mittens. A farm child learns early not to touch metal with a bare hand. Adult or youngster cannot relax vigilance.

Frostbite is the enemy. The enemy can also attack skiers and hikers. Skin freezes in varying degrees, like burning; in first-degree frostbite the nose or fingers are cold, white, and numb. Warmed, the skin looks reddish and burned. In second-degree cases, warmed skin will blister. In third degree, the skin has a livid dusky look and pain is intense; there has been loss of skin and subcutaneous tissues. Skin frostbitten in the fourth degree cannot be warmed, but remains dark and lifeless; entire fingers or toes or feet must be amputated.

If frostbite occurs, the injured skin must be treated gently and warmed with moderate rapidity—against the body heat of a companion, or in applications of warm water. The old folklore remedy—rubbing with snow—can be lethal, as can the too-intense heat of a fire. The human skin can freeze quickly, but must be patiently and gradually brought back to life.

January 10

Nature persists and lingers, always at the edges of civilization and creeping subtly inwards, even in the grimiest town, the sootiest city. It is impossible to seal up the chinks altogether. Animals, more willing than man to seek out survival and shelter at the cost of discomfort, take chances in their accommodations, sometimes living right under the noses of their human relatives. These country cousins intrude:

Near the outskirts of Seattle, two coyotes hunt for food in a gravel pit. Just their tracks during the day, and at dusk they can be seen as loping shadow shapes on scrub-covered hills. In January, chilly rattlesnakes crawl down from the hills around Los Angeles to warm themselves by unoccupied swimming pools. Birds persist and multiply, even when unwanted, unwelcome, and totally out of habitat; a motorist stalled in New York City traffic had the heart-jarring surprise of a hawk flying into the car window. Squirrels are familiar, pigeons decorate parks and sparrows nest where they obviously shouldn't—according to man's view. Despite being hunted, shot on sight, named as a desperado and set against bulls for entertainment, grizzly bears persist in lingering on; an unaccountable few survivors have wandered down from Canada into North Cascades National Park. A wild dog cannily scratches for existence in Central Park, with an inflamed look in his eye, hiding from manicured poodles and their owners. Roadbanks are cut down and trees chopped off and stumps hauled away, to build the concrete veins of the city; yet crews know that they must continually spray the raw soil with chemicals or stubborn life will spring up again.

January 11

Overnight, a silver thaw. The most dramatic of changes has occurred. Snow melted under rain, and then the temperature dropped again, and the world turned silver. Solid ice hangs like weights on branches and power lines and buildings. Frozen into white shapes like a glass-wired cage, the world has a look of permanence, a total fixation in this brittle process. Trees are white painted trees, immobile and artificial.

Sudden silver thaws cripple power lines, freeze water pipes, crush roofs. Without electricity or water, confined by lethal icy roads, families resort to primitive and makeshift methods of survival, struggling with heating food over fireplaces and chipping at blocks of ice to melt water, huddling in blankets in a sorry semblance of stoicism.

In the discomfort and stress of these few days before the temperature relents, there is an interval of the purest sort of beauty, glittering and astonishing to the eye, a dazzling, eye-jarring world of impersonal white.

January 12

The fine art of snow camping—making comfort out of discomfort—is best practiced on a mild winter afternoon when the weather is in a settled period (not always a predictable event). A good deal of energy goes into making a useful and tolerable camp, that would in the summer be expended in hiking and scrambling, but this is part of the game—and the fun.

The key to snow camping is insulation. A variety of things can be interposed between the sleeper and the snow: air mattress, clothing, packboards—even a climbing rope wrapped in sweater and parka can act as a pillow. The best bed is a foam pad topped by clothing.

A tree cave, the conical depression formed in the snow around a tree trunk, makes a fine shelter with its canopy of protective branches. A tarp can be hung to supplement the natural roof. The tent is placed on a stamped-out platform slightly larger than the tent floor (with a cautious eye on the weather, campers may dig out drainage ditches). A small area in front of the tent is also stamped out for easy exit and return. A whiskbroom, and a strict practice of using it to brush snow off boots and clothing, helps insure a dry tent.

Dinner begins early as dusk rises from the horizon and fills in the sky. Preferably, the stove is placed in the zippered opening of the tent floor, on the ground. Even in a well-ventilated tent, a good deal of warmth can be gotten from a stove and a plumber's candle.

Since the evening inside the tent is long, dinner begins early and consists of several small courses. Soup is a nourishing and reassuring beginning; from there one progresses to various possibilities, depending on how far the camper is from the car. Winter provides its own refrigeration and canny campers have carried hamburgers, mixed potatoes and peas, and even a shortcake of pound cake and bananas. Cocoa is a soothing top-off.

Night takes over a snow-filled forest, altering and subduing the lines of trees and slopes so that the entire landscape seems to float in a suspended Japanese-like vista of delicacy and insubstantiality. Stars are an extra bonus. The camper withdraws into his snug sleeping bag, squirrellike, socks curled near his feet, and leaves an open space around his face, quite comfortably putting himself into a temporary hibernation.

The benefits of snow camping are a perverse delight in overcoming the mild discomforts of chill and wet, and in waking—surprisingly early—to view minute by minute a glittering, ice castle world, becoming rose pink and grateful under a tardy winter sun.

January 14

There is a silence to nature, a reticence, most noticeable now in midwinter, in the deep of the year. The earth's ornamentation is stripped away and the earth, in its essentials, is silent. On a January noon, woods and fields in their stillness seem withdrawn, and remote. What is more apparent now is the total uncommunicativeness of the natural world, the mystery.

There is a dignity to the earth, even its most abandoned processes. Nature conceals and protects, even in the midst of the gamboling processes of lovemaking and reproduction, the flying seeds, the shout of birds. No secrets come from nature; what is learned has to be pried forth, measured, analyzed, and—ultimately—guessed.

The final mystery is the silence. Butterflies do not speak. Plants, sensitive and aware as they may be as living organisms, responding to temperature and light, are more than stamen and pistil and pollen, but have no messages for man. Thornton Wilder commented that the best thing about animals is that they don't speak much. The world goes on in quiet despite man's interference, and the ultimate questions are never answered.

Nature subdues. Even the most careless and stupid of men fall silent in the presence of great mysteries—sequoia trees, great canyons. Men who live long in the presence of nature seem to lose their own ready voices. Farmers are succinct and naturalists become taciturn, and tentative in their answers. Men who have lived in the wilderness any length of time find themselves with little to say; they weigh their occasional words and speak haltingly.

The wisest observers of nature are probably those who simply listen, who cease their own clamor, and wait for the break in the silence.

January 15

The gray whales begin their annual migration from the Arctic to the breeding grounds of lower California lagoons. From now to April great numbers of these leviathans will move down the coast on their 4,000-mile journey.

Oddly, though the gray whale, like other whales, has been persecuted and hunted, the whales move companionably near the shore, plainly visible even to cars on the highway at certain points along the southern California coast.

The whales hardly have time to eat. They are busy with the processes of mating and calving. Some females are wallowing in shallow water, bearing sixteen-foot calves; others are mating. Males are in the majority, but the business of reproduction proceeds without fights.

These are immense barnacle-encrusted animals, at least forty feet in length, weighing up to forty tons or more. Females are the largest. They have a surprising look of gentleness, even when viewed fairly close, although they have been called devilfish, for their playful custom of bumping boats.

Whale watching has become great sport, since protective laws have halted shooting of the great gray beasts. Boat operators run a thriving business of daily whale-watching trips.

Premium entertainment when a forty-five-foot, forty-ton whale breaches within twenty yards of a boat, perhaps repeating the spectacular leap four or five times, like a performer with a sense of fey humor. Humans, gaping from cars, beaches, and boat decks, seem to be watching and often appear absorbed and observant, though human behavior is not always easy to evaluate.

January 16

Birds have been associated with death, symbols both of approaching death and the fleeing soul, but in winter stillness the sounds of their calling are welcome proof of life. Nothing is more fully alive than a bird; vocal, agile, bouncy, intensely wakeful, birds possess the total vibrancy of livingness. Feeding birds in winter is a happy task. A frozen birdbath has to be chipped free of ice. Suet and bread crumbs are appreciated additions to the feeder, along with the normal stock of wild bird seed. Once the responsibility of feeding wintering birds is accepted it must be continued; birds are guests who know a good thing when they see it. The repayment is more than generous; a crowd of chattering birds on a winter morning say that winter is an illusion and spring not far away.

January 17

Insects have found their winter homes. As larvae, some are snug inside cases made of silk and pubescences of leaves; the cases may be surprisingly shaped—those of the pistol case bearer or the cigar case bearer, for example. On the bare branches of trees and shrubs, the large silky cocoon of the cecropia moth is conspicuous. The silken tent is a strong durable structure, with an outer and an inner wall; in between are random strands of silk that provide insulating air spaces. Frayed cattail heads serve as winter homes for cattail moths.

These are serviceable quarters, protecting the larvae from extremes of temperature and moisture.

Adult insects seek out shelter in a variety of places. In the fields, the beetles, weevils, leafhoppers and aphis lions live among the roots of grasses and other plants. In grasslands, hornets winter in sphagnum moss. Wasps have found homes in fences and in stone walls; flies and mosquitoes wait out the winter in niches of houses and barns.

The woods are home for wintering insects—decaying logs are well populated with beetles and fireflies and wireworms; even salamanders and spiders live here. On the forest floor itself, tenants are comfortably housed under the insulating dead leaves; spiders, snails and worms share the protecting warmth.

The silverfish, delicate and pretty in color, elusive in habit, is a persistent guest in houses, for it has a troublesome liking for books and papers; it has been an unwelcome resident of libraries and museums.

Ice-filled streams are chilly residences for species of the stone fly, who complete their nymphal lives here and take to the air to mate. The young of the stone fly, the naiads, cling to the undersides of rocks in the flowing water.

Hiding, waiting, in their subtle places of concealment, the insects pass the winter. The months will go by and insects—summer's living dust—will gather again in the air, will again populate the ground.

January 18

Nature is fond of circles: planets, stars, raindrops, snowflakes (perfect hexagons of crystal shaped within the circle), the round dome of horizon. Of all nature's patterns, the circle occurs most often, and life itself reflects a circular process, the unbroken ring of birth and death and eternity.

January 19

The animals sleep.

Hibernation has occurred for millions of years and is still a strange, little understood process. It is a magic trick but the sleight of hand is never revealed. A near-death stage of withdrawal and catatonia, it also protects the animal; a hibernating creature is invulnerable to pain, for hibernation is also anaesthesia and a protective device to enable the animal to sleep unharmed by things that would normally kill.

The Indians called it the long sleep, but it is more than sleep, a total slowing down of all the bodily processes. Circulation slows, blood is stiffened and sluggish, the heart beats at a slow fractional pace, temperature drops. Digestion virtually stops in many animals, who will wake in the spring with last autumn's meal still in their stomachs, unconsumed. Kidneys and bladder cease to function. In deep slumber, a hibernator has been proved immune to poisons and drowning.

For all practical purposes, a hibernating animal has gone away for the winter. A trick of adaptation enables it to survive cold, scarcity of food, and lethal storms as surely as if it had fled; only the retreat is to within itself, a rigid torpor of closure and denial.

They all sleep now: the bears in their dens (they doze, actually), the rattlesnakes twined in communal sharing of warmth and slumber, the bats hanging upside down in comfortless caves, frogs at the bottom of ponds, snails, chipmunks, squirrels, gophers. All are plunged into the comatose depth, held as rigidly as if intoxicated or poisoned. Marmots sleep in underground chambers when snow covers the meadows where they frolicked.

Perfect hibernator is the woodchuck, who in the fall grows round and fat as his hour of drowsiness approaches.

Now he sleeps and slowly, slowly the fat burns; he will wake in the spring skimpy-light with a third of that fuel consumed. He has no dreams; his brain is a void.

But he will wake swiftly; blood races to the brain, waking it, and then to body organs, and their temperature rapidly rises. Violent shivering and panting arouse the animal fully in as little as two hours. Abruptly he returns to the world.

Like migration, hibernation seems a miracle; it is the original energy-saving ruse. Impossible to say exactly what triggers the escape—not temperature alone, or diminishing light, or scarcity of food.

A comparable instinct may exist in man, who once too was a cold-blooded animal. Faced with winter, many people feel a primeval longing to give up the fight, to turn away from the urgencies of survival.

People sleep later in the mornings, turn in earlier at night, stay in the shelter of their homes.

Hibernation is a taste of death—or perhaps, eternity; the cool and witless sleep freed of the cravings of ambition and the fever of fear, safe from pain and death.

January 20

Norsemen believed they were the lanterns of savage maidens looking for likely prey. American Indians considered them the fires of brave warriors lighted over the bodies of victims. On clear, cold nights in the Dakotas and northern states the lights appear in the sky and the show begins, the silent brilliant dance of the lights.

At times the aurora borealis hangs like a moving bank of draperies, shifting, billowing, a curtain coldly on fire. At other times, the northern lights dance and dart in the sky; rays of color leap up, fall back, and dart ahead again. Or the entire sky fills with vivid streamers of light. Red and green flash against the yellow-white bands, as the lights pulsate and shimmer.

The spectacle of the cold-blazing lights is accomplished in perfect silence and has a weird, alien look, as if a hundred visiting gods of the sky waved and flashed their lights in a frenzied dance.

As suddenly as it began, the lights may die down, and only a weak, pale illumination colors the sky, barely moving and gradually subsiding altogether.

Unlike the rainbow, which is an illusion of reflected light, the northern lights arise from the horizon as tiny particles released from the sun enter the earth's atmosphere, arriving at speeds of thousands of miles a second. The electrically charged particles, meeting and funneled by the earth's magnetic field, excite the air molecules, some six hundred miles high, into luminescence. At their most spectacular, the lights begin as a glow on the northern horizon and kindle the night in a leaping arc of color, as if the runaway sun burned a hole in the sky.

January 21

A SUDDEN SPRING

Now and then in January an unaccountable warm day as a full-bodied sun comes out and temperatures rise. The reprieve takes the sting out of winter; a temporary halt calls an end to cold wind and snow flurries, and the damp heavy chill of winter. The day is totally springlike, wildly out of season; men walk around in shirtsleeves and smile more often, like children let out of school at recess.

January 22

Blizzards strike and paralyze the earth. Lasting up to three days or more, a blizzard can halt all activity, freezing and crippling entire towns. The survivors of Donner Pass remembered a white anguished world; years later, a passenger train was forced to a halt on the same route and its cars buried in whirling drifts of snow, its riders held like captives.

Snow, swept and carved by driving winds, can travel with ferocious speed, piling in high drifts and banks, burying automobiles and reaching up the doorways of houses. In the peak of a blizzard, what began as a gentle snowstorm—a paperweight flurry—becomes a twisting, howling fury that wears a mask; the world is opaque. People struggling to reach shelter in the midst of a blizzard have fallen in these swirling clouds, clutched at choking snow-filled winds, and frozen to death a hundred feet from safety.

Finally the storm ceases. The blizzard is past. It is a white silent world of grotesque forms and bizarre fancies—cars drunkenly perched off roadways, snow taller than a man's head piled against a shed, a King's X of bare ground beside the windbreak of a grain elevator.

During a storm, people become more tense, excited, possibly more intelligent (IQ scores have been shown to rise in periods of electrical activity). After the storm, people are exhilarated, gazing out on the crystalline and quieted world. They have now another memory that will grow and ripen with the years, like a personal vision of their own endurance and immensity: "Remember the great blizzard?"

January 23

Winter has sharp hard edges. Trees have brittle bones and occasionally a branch cracks under the weight of snow. Ice crackles along the edges of roads and lakes. Voices carry farther, and more distinctly.

There is a clarity to winter, both to the eye and ear. Mountains, bold-postured, take up aggressive stances against the sky. Twilights are firm strokes of black and white, and the land has a lean look. A winter moon is bold and bright.

January 25

THE GAP

An unimaginable, therefore unbridgeable, gap exists between man and say, an anemone, or a periwinkle, or a bee, or a Joshua pine, or an eagle. Yet these too live, have memories, respond.

A periwinkle, moving inland on the sands, retains a memory of the tides in its grasping and feeding habits. In contrast, man seems a creature with amnesia. A plant may be considered sensitive—that is, it often seems to respond to stimuli of light or sound, or a repeated disturbance of an energy pattern may provoke the plant like a memory. An eagle will claim the sky for ten miles around as his territory, and quote its boundaries exactly—in the circling flight or the leap of attack.

In some sensitivity courses, a person may place himself inside a flower and imagine himself growing up and out, leafing, climbing the dimness of the green stalk to get a handhold on the sun; yet it is unthinkable that a plant "knows" where it is going. To imagine a rudimentary consciousness inside leaves and stems would be to imagine the most confined of confinements. What, for that matter, would it be like to be a moss on a log? Sensitivity fails. All that can be suspected is a nothingness; yet the moss grows in search of light, and it is this growing which nags at the mind. Some species of plants and animals seem the crudest kind of machinery, and yet, inexplicably, grow. The growing is what counts, or, more precisely, the being; to be is to imply the possibility of change, of *not being*. The crudest slime mold, or the zipping hummingbird, are engaged in being; each has a share of the mystery and the potentiality. Some people regard plants and animals as totally alien, uninhabited devices. They do not consider that there is a gap at all, which is to say that they are unaware of any connection.

January 27

On a snow-covered mountain slope, a ptarmigan is the color of snow. The bird represents a striking example of adaptation for survival by camouflage, and other adjustments. The bird has plumed feet, enabling it to move with ease on snow, and is densely feathered—a snug winter resident, making its diet on moss and lichen, and scraps of twigs and pine needles. Glimpsed now and then by skiers and hikers, the bird has an easy elegance; a drab summertime grouse becomes beautiful and dignified in its winter dress. Adaptation by color is one of nature's many tricks. The pepper moth in England that survived by color, changing to the sooty shade of air-polluted and blackened trees, is also a barometer of civilization's impact on nature; where pollution has been controlled and the trees healed, the paler speckled moth is once more reappearing—industrial melanism turned full circle.

January 29

The true paths of history are the rivers.

Great rivers opened the routes of exploration, taking the early travelers to unguessed destinations, opening views to lands they had not known existed, determining the courses of rude trails and of modern highways. Rivers carry in their veins the commerce and adventure of men, but are also the homes of animals and fish, feed hydroelectric dams, are the battlefields of the conservationists and the at-all-costs producers; in their descent from the glaciers until they spill in the sea, rivers carve the way of destiny.

The great Columbia, 1,214 miles in length, follows south and west from southeastern British Columbia through Washington state, and pursues between Oregon and Washington its long route to the Pacific Ocean. It carries in its river-voice the names of men and stone and water: Beacon Rock, Astor, McLoughlin, Multnomah Falls. Rich in somber and splendid history, the river is for much of its length, in January, wrapped in rich gray fog.

Captain Robert Grey, fur trader, in 1792 discovered Greys Harbor, crossed the bar, and carrying a letter of endorsement from

George Washington, entered long-sought Oregon, thus entitling the United States, by right of discovery, to the vast region drained by the river and its tributaries. In honor of the event, the river was named for the *Columbia*, the ship that first carried the American flag around the world.

The river was "Wauna" to the Chinook Indians, "La Roque" to the Spaniards, "River of the West" to the French. Lewis and Clark followed the river across Oregon to the Pacific. Forts and fur trading companies were established along the Columbia; men like white-bearded Dr. John McLoughlin, paternal figure (a stern one) to the Indians, and Captain Bonneville, or Astor, knew its possibilities and its dangers. Reverend Jason Lee preached to the Indians at The Dalles Mission on the Columbia, then sold the mission to Dr. Marcus Whitman, who with his wife had traveled the Columbia to the Northwest. Later, at the mission near Walla Walla, their child, the "little papoose," was drowned in the Walla Walla River, and the Whitmans killed in an Indian massacre, retribution for epidemic measles and a perhaps less than understanding treatment. Marcus Whitman stands as Oregon's ultimate martyr and his bride the purest heroine. Fair Narcissa! For that frail stubborn girl, so terrifyingly concerned for Indian souls and body cleanliness, the Columbia and the Walla Walla were paths to a sorely attained glory.

Beacon Rock stands not far east of Portland, a great dark monolith, a test for rock climbers who ignore the easy trail that spirals up to splendid views. Multnomah Falls, a solitary grand leap of water, is commercialized by the usual restaurant and gift shop.

Oregon was truly an empire at one time—a land of limitless furs and wealth, a green mist-drenched kingdom with counties as big as European nations, a land to nurture human pride and greed. The Columbia has been home to beaver and salmon. Homeric journeys of the salmon are famous; thousands of the fish, born in the Columbia, travel to the sea and then take the long journey back, relentlessly bound for the destination of their first home, there to spawn and die. It has been reasonably well established that salmon find their way back to home— their birthplace and deathplace—by means of smell, among possible other factors. Great thousands of these glittering, leaping bodies were sport and food for Indians on slippery platforms poised above the river; now, dams and construction have greatly reduced the number of fish. In winter, the Columbia seems a gray and fog-held river, no playground, a scene for martyrs and conquerors and poets.

January 31

Winter is thought of as a pause, a time of retreat, and of waiting. The seeds that fell last August are supposedly dormant. Yet not altogether dormant, these too are acted on by the season. Many seeds need this period of cold before they can sprout. Winter is also a time of growth, and a part of the entire complex process, but the changes occurring now are subtle and unseen. On chilly ground, under snow perhaps, the seeds are alive and in the act of becoming; the thrust of cold and dark are as necessary to the scheme as light and warmth. In the rough circles of seed shapes life is staked out; the property of life itself is claimed.

February 1

Patterns for February: Bare antlers of trees. The close gray bowl of the sky. Clouds like low-drawn curtains. Frost circles on windows.

February 2

Fashions in animal lore occur, just as in animal fur (generally now in bad taste, at least with the more enlightened). Just as hunters used to eat the hearts of lions for courage, men later adorned their womenfolk with spotted coats or mink or hung dead hummingbirds on their hats, by a process of transference proving their own prowess and asserting a claim to beauty and power. Some bits of animal lore persist. A friendly folktale is the wisdom attributed to the groundhog, supposed prophet of spring, and newspaper and TV broadcasters still make ritualistic nods in his direction: did he or did he not see his shadow?

Animal fortunes often rise and fall on the most witless of arbitrary decisions (the coyote is too smart for his own good, pandas are lately lovable). The owl has been popular; now the cycle seems to be shifting toward the raccoon. Some animals—snakes, spiders—never win any popularity contest, remaining obstinately unlovable, and few people "care for" skunks or porcupines. The wallflowers of the animal world far outweigh the chosen, much as in human populations; so-called minority groups are by far the world's majority. (Evolution apparently picks and chooses on a fairer basis, an argument for the unlucky that the meek will inherit the earth.)

February 2 appearances usually are a chancy gamble, but the groundhog has the odds weighted in his favor; winter's and spring's clocks govern the clock mechanisms of the sleeping animals and the hidden seeds. The pendulum continues to swing.

February 3

February is everything a month shouldn't be. It is wet, sodden, chilled. Snows lie deep and immovable in the woods. Storm follows on storm. The sky is gray wool, wringing wet. Wind shears off branches. Skunk cabbage, stolidly wet-footed, raises its head, scenting the air with its blunt, rank-onion, almost fetid smell.

There is little to love in February's obstinate down-to-the-depths grayness and dimness, a blurry, underwater look of rain-swimming fields, the chill heavy skies, a short handspan of capricious twilight. An occasional sunny day is tantalizing rather than satisfying.

As if winter weren't long enough, February shows no overt sign of improvement. Lakes and rivers are frozen and the brief relenting thaw may be followed by an angry blizzard.

Earthworms are waiting it out, packed in close patient balls below the frost line to conserve body moisture. Animals are in retreat, many of them observing the dreary silence of February. Water worms and insects, most unprepossessing and colorless of life forms, seem the only signs of activity in the sluggish snows: the winter snow fly, the diving beetle, lace bug. Leeches cling in sedentary fashion to the undersides of rocks in fast brooks; *Asellus communis*, a tiny model of an armadillo, moves sluggishly among the decayed leaves and mud of woodland pools. Scuds, flea-size acrobats, perform their jerky stunts, and are snatched and swallowed by brook trout.

Dark and dreary February is the moody hiatus, the gap between the pure white depths of January and the soon-to-burgeon wild activity of March.

Unlovable February in its sullen pessimism is mercifully also the shortest month.

February 7

A good day for studying seed catalogs. Throughout the country, people are entertaining grandiose illusions and fond hopes, transporting themselves to a bright and flowery future as they thumb through the familiar pages of this most magical of wishbooks.

The darker and grayer the day, the brighter the well-loved illustrations. Too early to plant most seeds, but flowers have sat for their portraits:

Campanula: Carpalica Blue; a radiant array of hanging silent bells.

Hollyhock: paper lanterns with a solidly reassuring, old-fashioned look. Nostalgia comes in vivid shades of pink and deep rose-red.

Marigold: pale yellow to gold to assertive bold orange, so lively and confident in their colors that their piquant scent seems to leap sharply from the page. Marigolds are said to keep down nematodes, and, planted near cabbage and beans, discourage rabbits.

Who could resist the promise of candy-striped zinnia, "as luscious as it sounds: Full round flowers striped bright pink, rose or cerise on a white background . . . large well-doubled flowers on bushy plants provide a varied display midsummer to frost. Each flower, thick and full with artistically ruffled petals radiates every ray of light to glow in the summer sun."

Surely this will be the summer when flowers bloom and burst in abundance, when the garden sings with color, when the yard will be the envy of neighbors.

Fingers turning the pages itch, and outside the gray darkness of February slants down close at the windows, the cautious, hold-back, wait-awhile fingers of winter.

Flowers have a calling, though in their profusion of color and scent, they have still a charming reticence, part of nature's reserved behavior as to purpose or plan.

Flower seed capital of the world is Lompoc, California, producing over 80 percent of the Free World's flower seeds. A combination of dense dark riverbottom loam and long rainless summers, cooled by ocean breezes, makes the ideal environment for growing seeds. A young man in England, Silas Cole, attended a tea party at the home of Lady Spencer, and noted a new and alluring sweet pea blossom. The flower grew sporadically under England's chilly rains. Cole wrote enthusiastically to W. Atlee Burpee. This was in 1901. In 1907 a young Scotsman, John Smith, suggested to a bean farmer in Lompoc, Robert D. Rennie, that he try growing sweet peas. Rennie planted a prospering half-acre. Later a bean seed buyer from Burpee brought together W. Atlee Burpee, who remembered the seeds sent to him from England by Silas Cole, and farmer Rennie, and from this slight beginning grew a flourishing industry—without a doubt the most beautiful business in the world.

February 8

The month is one of the doldrums. Bills. The ague. Complaints. (Delayed mail, unanswered letters, high cost of fuel, windows need new weatherstripping.) The garden has a devastated look. Even house pets seem to share in their owners' impatient irritability or loss of gladness; a surly tomcat goes in wailing search of a sexual romp. Best remedy for the doldrums: a walk around a winter-stopped lake at the edge of the woods. Deciduous trees are bare, or what few leaves remain are olive drab, an army in retreat.

There is punishment in the slap of chilly air, total absence or fragments only of view, even the unproductive scene of arrested growth. In the stillness, the occasional keening of a bird is simply punctuation. All the same, the walk is more than a chastening exercise or a disciplinary practice in self-restraint.

The trees are black and white line drawings. All of nature is stripped down to the subtlest of meanings and forms, seems to be saying, Now what?

Now endures. At the crux of the desolation is the permanence; the hard scaffolding of nature shows through. The structure will survive the seasons.

Without the garish colors and scents of summer, mad May blooms like Ophelia with flowers in her hair, the pore-opening assault of

August, nature is a cross-tempered and frugal landlady who has turned off the heat. Tenants do with what scraps of comfort they can find: mountain climbers slog a short ways up snow-covered roads, gardeners look for signs of life and take the pulse of the soil, birdwatchers refill the tree feeder, and carry bits of suet along to lure the birds at the lake.

There is said to be an exhilaration or a surcease in a winter's walk; a primal appetite is satisfied in venturing from the mouth of the cave and returning wet and chilled, vaguely stronger and pleased with oneself.

February 10

Cabin fever is still a genuine ailment with isolated individuals in Alaska or remote mountain homes or prairie outposts. Being snowbound for any period of time is a pretty spectacle in imagination alone—the reading of poems by the fire, eating last year's bounty, the silent communion with self. February is low on sensory stimuli, repetitive in its melancholy, and even people in cities become irritable and impatient. Even with no lack of human companionship, humans show signs of temper and become dour and unwilling. The human heart is in need of green.

Individuals blanketed, masked and muffled and put in isolation rapidly become both schizophrenic and paranoid, claim that their heads are floating away from their bodies and their thought sequences jumbling like disorderly boxcars shuffled onto a siding. To a lesser degree, people sitting and staring out wet darkened windows become a little crazy. What they are looking for actually is not more company or bridge parties or any human activity, but the green resurgence of the non-human. The senses crave the sound of birds and the green of buds and, above all, light.

February 11

Porridge is for dark winter mornings in the low times of the pendulum's swing. A homely solid reassurance to grains and cereals, and the more old-fashioned and plain the better. (Pioneers would have distrusted sugar crispies.) There is something basic and satisfying to a bowl of hot oatmeal or simply mush, eaten with sugar and milk. The fires of winter days are stoked with the harvest of summer.

February 12

A good thing to brighten February days is the air fern. Small (four to five inches) and feathery green, the plant resembles any young species of garden or house plant. Actually, it is a form of plant life that requires no water, soil, or feeding, simply air—and the moisture in the air. Its normal habitat is along the banks of the English Channel, and on the coast of Ireland.

Standing in a vase or cup, it makes no apparent overt demands whatever on the environment. Day after day, it is the same ungrowing miniature (actually it will become a trifle larger) and unchanging green, a plant of delicacy and modesty to put in dark corners or empty spots, a living ornament with an elfish leprechaun look. It appears not to grow or change whatever, but if moved to a hostile environment—for example, smog-ridden areas of Los Angeles—it turns brown and shrivels and dies.

February 14

Valentine of the marshlands is the redwing. Premature sign of spring, it ventures back from the southern states. Males come first; old birds lead the way ahead of the young ones. With blazing red shoulders, the birds sing a liquid song to match their watery setting. The dead sodden brown of the marshes fills with sound and color and flash of movement.

All action, the pioneer male wins and stakes his territory, homesteading in vigorous action against the time, a few weeks later, when the females will come.

Love is a reproductive instinct, and the wish for home life a temper display of plotting the lot lines, but the swooping dashing redwing wears the scarlet epaulets of affection's symbolic color; his heart is on his sleeve.

February 15

For some, this is the mating season. Water isopods begin their long breeding period; the female will be continually pregnant, producing a new batch of young every five or six weeks. Skunks and squirrels choose mates, yellow perch migrate to the shallows of ponds and lake shores to spawn, the great horned owl makes a noisy hooting business of his wooing. The female owl stubbornly incubates on the coldest days and nights, even to sitting on the eggs under a snow blanket. Snow flies mate. Normally aloof and diffident, the woodcock chooses this one unpromising month to sing its mating song. The flicker, in a rapture to excess, tattoos at a limb like a savage drummer calling for his love.

February 16

The bare and skinny tree branches have the look of antlers. Matching these austere patterns, elk roam through deep snow in search of food—scarce in winter. Grass is hidden, leaves are gone, there is no longer enough for everyone.

Each winter, thousands of elk will die; others in some areas will live simply because cougars and wolves—their summer enemies—are gone. Nature is as much absence as presence, starvation as plenty, pain as pleasure. Competition is desperate now in the lowlands for what food can be found.

In some parks and reserves, air drops to the dying animals, not a gesture of simple sentimentality, but ultimately a matter of human survival—keeping part of the food chain alive, the circle unbroken. Care packages to animals seem the most absurd of incongruities, opposed to careless feedings by summer tourists and the autumn hunt, yet may make up a little for the thoughtlessness, be a partial recompense, trying to patch up the pieces and tilt the balance again. Kindly or vicious, man is an inordinate meddler.

February 17

On Sunday, February 17, 1907, the Seattle Mountaineers had their first outing. Forty-eight members and guests met at 9:30 A.M. to hike to the West Point Lighthouse and lunch over a campfire. Both men and women wore hats, and the ladies wore long skirts.

An unpretentious beginning for a club that has since grown strong—some eight thousand members concerned both with mountaineering and conservation.

In its early days the club reflected almost entirely the shadow of one man's personality: its second and long-time president, Edmond Stephen Meany.

In the classroom at the University of Washington, Meany was a professor with a historian's zeal (he had helped establish historic statues and monuments throughout the state); in the mountains Meany was a missionary with just as fervent a calling: educating clumsy city folk to the wonders of trees and snow-capped peaks.

Washington State was still half-frontier, nervously becoming civilized; people felt self-conscious about their beautiful rain-drenched forests and fog-hidden mountains. It was a novelty to explore and climb; the wilderness of the Olympics lay just beyond the doorstep, and the wilds seemed inexhaustible.

To these wanderers, Meany imparted the message of the mountains, in Indian legends told around the campfires, in poetry too sentimental for modern tastes, in calls to prayer in alpine settings.

Scholarly (Meany wrote a *History of Washington State* and compiled an impressive *Origin of Washington Geographic Names*), he was still professor on the trail, even in rough clothes and boots. Tall, austere-looking, with a formidable reddish beard, he seldom lost his dignity or his air of leadership, whether crossing a log over a river or admitting to a group of followers that somehow the trail seemed lost.

An idealist, Meany was a friend of John Muir, and friend to nature, without ever fully realizing the responsibility and hazard of such a devotion. "We are learning to avail ourselves of the automobiles as we will of the airplane in time. None of them can ever destroy the lure of the trail and the camp at timber's edge."

Meany climbed no really big mountains—and he was not the first to climb the peak named for him in the Olympics—but he forged and nurtured the early Mountaineer philosophy as surely as if the Mountaineers were another class group, blocking a proposed outing to Alaska, encouraging the building of an agate and concrete block structure over hot springs at Mount Rainier National Park.

Between outings and classes, he composed literally hundreds of poems, some of which are fairly bad, and all rather touching: "Be sure, my soul, this faith to keep, climbing the mountain's rugged steep."

They went to Mount Rainier, to Mount Baker, to Mount Stuart. Meany preached, cajoled, lectured, his arms waving with enthusiasm over a frosty sunrise or a sleeping giant of an unconquered peak. The Mountaineers, for all the hats and skirts, were a hardy and impetuous band of individualists who gathered around the campfire at night to tell of horrific climbs, nerve-shattering rock scrambles, perils of rivers to ford—and ate lustily of the camp cook's efforts. Not much was said about conservation, or the impact of a party of a hundred plus people descending on frail mountain meadows; wouldn't those glorious days last forever? Edmond Meany read a goodnight poem as the campfire dwindled.

With his death, the club faltered, went on, and became an impressive organization, highly conservation-conscious, often plagued with the usual bureaucratic ills. A fierce-eyed portrait in the clubroom watches a succession of presidents.

It is a long ways from the mass outings and the happy innocent philosophy of the history professor. Few Mountaineers today know of Meany more than his name, and feel less curiosity.

Still, a girl walking around camp on a summer evening in the Olympics a couple of years ago was startled when she saw a tall figure standing on the rocks, hat in hand, bearded face uplifted, in a poet's stance. The beard, she thought, was red; she couldn't be sure because she looked away and when she looked back the figure was gone.

February 18

A month of roots and water. February is the time to plant root crops—potatoes, carrots—and water is everywhere, where there is no snow. Roots seem an essential foundation, a statement of life and of belonging, but are actually latecomers; the first forms of life come from the water. Water is still baptism and renewal, and the original source; unchanged insects and fish throng in the ponds and rivers, and the human body itself is largely composed of water. The dolphin and the whale, some believe, have brains like their bodies, large, mysterious, capable of undiscovered function.

Man himself is a cunning predator-politician risen from humble origins, possibly the volcano-warmed shores of Lake Rudolf. Here he hunted with an astonishing number of frail contemporaries;

Cain and Abel may have been cannibals without knowing it, animal species who did not recognize in each other the common bent, the taboo of the resemblance. From the lifeless strata, fragments of skulls and femurs with their odd, distressing implications: the large brain case remarkably early in the game, the something—or someone—who had emerged from the waters, walked erect with limbs rooted to the earth, vanished irretrievably in some species and without burial, yet assertive and permanent in the jigsaw puzzle of his bones, proving that "man" is not an entity but a concept.

February 19

Snowshoeing is a highly civilized art, originally practiced by primitives—that is, settlers and trappers in inhospitable environments who by necessity learned the discipline and control necessary for confident and comfortable snowshoe travel.

Occasionally, a February day is clear and bright—a pallid windowpane that suggests a look ahead to the bright open days of spring. Then the low-hanging clouds like birds fly away and an unseasonal warmth deceptively softens the somber outlines of winter-bound woods.

Bear-paw snowshoes are good for short tramps, or easy maneuvering where the going is steep and brushy; the longer cross-country or trail snowshoes adapt the hiker to more venturesome rambles and lonely travel. Rawhide is the traditional lacing, the preferred choice when treated with a good marine varnish. Neoprene lacings, less aesthetically satisfying, are lighter, impervious to oils, and resistant to water or rodent damage. Nylon gaiters keep out snow.

Clothing—even on a warm bright February day—remains winter clothing; the snowshoer dresses for gales and snowstorms and remains mindful of early dark. The sweater and the light windbreaker is supplemented by the down parka in the pack; wool headgear and mittens, boots and wool socks are all necessities for the winter walk on webbed feet.

Elinor Wylie called them "velvet shoes." The velvet is in the surroundings, winter snows piled lightly or more deeply on logging roads and hidden trails. Actually, snowshoes produce a squeak—a soft reassuring sibilance of friendly sound as one foot slides past the other.

Novices try to lift the foot too much, or walk deliberately straddle-legged, and are soon complaining of cumbersome footgear and tired ankles—or worse, the effortful process of getting upright after a fall.

Snowshoeing is hard work. A snowshoer, exerting muscles and lungs, will be sweating as he travels. Only when he stops does he realize that February clarity is an illusion, the sun a chill and uncomforting thing in its remoteness. Seasoned snowshoers carry coffee or tea, or even a light butane stove to heat bouillon in the shelter of a tree.

Unlike the downhill skier, the snowshoer gets his rewards in slow motion. He has time to study the stencil tracks of birds, the record of a rabbit's crossing. Larger tracks invite curiosity and speculation, but the woods are still.

The great bonus of snowshoeing is silence. On a February day in the woods, sounds are few, and are magnified, just as the winter sunlight plays tricks on the eye, seeming to put mountains or landmark trees in unfamiliar locations.

Now a branch creaks, there is a soft thud as snow drops to the ground. A few birds chatter, cautious of human intrusion. In some parts of the country, a lucky snowshoer might catch a glimpse of a wolf—stare returning stare has a craggy look, a stern permanence like a rock mountain. Wolves have a brute dignity, intelligence masked in fur and bone, eyes that seem motionless and spacious.

More often, the traveler will surprise a ptarmigan—still dressed in winter white—or a camp robber, his beak stuffed with snow, hopefully on the lookout for handouts.

The marmot (that spring alarm clock of the mountains) and the bear are still sleeping. In February the woods have an arrested look of stillness and quiescence. Mountains repeating themselves in the distance are blue carbon copies of real mountains. The gray and white trees stand in inkpools of shadow on the snow.

In actuality, nature is never static; movement is incessant. Streams run underneath the temporary snow-bridges. Deer and fox work harder for a living. The snowshoer must be alert for his personal widowmakers—unexpectedly dropping lumps of hard snow, rocks concealed underfoot, tangle of prickly devil's club, the slippery log under the snow that will pitch him headlong.

Later, he returns to the highway and noise and voices. A February day ends quickly.

February 20

Colds and illnesses sprout in the winter like sodden fungi; everyone seems a festering incubator of dank and melancholy germs: the running nose, aching chest, prolific fevers. Despite all the vitamins and orange juice and sunlamps and flu shots in the world, people persist in getting ill. In the animal world, the hollow bodies of starvation; in well-fed human animals, the sickness of the cells.

Every winter, doctors make the same humorless pronouncement: colds and illnesses flourish only because of the crowded conditions of winter—people huddled in overheated office buildings to hide from the storm. This is a confusion of cause and effect.

In actuality, these are the low times of the spirit and the flesh, like the dark early hours of three and four in the morning—death hours for the human being. Winter—February—corresponds to just these unresisting hours when the barrier goes down.

Light is scarce and what comes through is peckish and disconsolate; a pale sun produces liverish days. Humans need light as much as food, and without it become depressed and find the germs always there in the air. A psychosomatic explanation is oversimplification, of course; bodies and cilia have to work harder to adjust to changes in temperature and humidity and have less energy to spare against the invasion of bacteria.

Still, the invalid turns watery eyes and streaming nose and eyes to the streaming skies; the old ones will die, most likely, if the winter is long and hard enough.

February 22

Ski touring is an escape from cocktail lounges, overheated lodges, jukeboxes, day nurseries, long lines at the ski lifts, sociable (and raucous) crowds under floodlighted slopes, banal chalets burgeoning on logged-off hills.

Ski touring is an escape to: silence, unpopulated glaciated terrain, unused logging roads, trees whitened with winter, snow that appears virginal and has a startling original look, like a blank canvas.

For the novice, the first experience of ski touring can be unsettling. The friendly lodge seems far away. Physical toil is required to take one up a slope, without the mechanical assistance of the lift. Landmarks are few on unplotted terrain and weather can be distressingly immediate. Unscheduled hazards appear with disturbing regularity. Without the competitive element of cross-country skiing—a highly specialized sport—or the neighborly bumptious scrambles of the crowded slopes, ski touring seems at first difficult and lonely. In actuality, it is a kind of artistry, requiring skill and patience; it is practiced for the simple joy of movement alone, in an untrodden environment.

Equipment is a major consideration. For anything more than the beginning trips, the special touring ski is desirable (not necessarily marketed under this name). This will be a deep-powder ski, possibly about twenty centimeters shorter than the recreational ski. Metal skis outlive wood. Uphill travel difficulties are eased by climbers and skins. A good climber is heavy black mohair bonded to strong canvas binding. For bindings, special touring toe pieces are available; cable forward throws are essential. Safety becomes an increasingly important consideration as the distance to the lodge increases. Touring poles should be chosen for strength and support rather than balance or fancy flexibility, and be short enough for ease in traversing.

Ski tourers of distinction dress for comfort and warmth: well-used downhill boots or special, insulated winter mountaineering boots, wool clothing in layers, cap, mittens, down parkas with hoods. A tourer feels no compulsion to be fashionable.

Without the benefits of lodge and lift, ski touring imposes the necessity of a rucksack to carry food and drink—and the precautionary items of maps and first aid essentials.

With acquired technique comes also the ability to judge weather and terrain, knowledge in navigation, and the ability to decide when retreat is the better part of valor. Glaciers can quite often be safely traveled in February, the same glaciers that soon will be death traps with partly concealed crevasses under the pressures of repeated thawing and refreezing, but are never highways.

Practice develops too, a self-sufficient confidence, and brings an odd sensation of not-alone pleasure. Solitary travel in the silent woods is the most companionable of experiences.

February 23

Winter picnics are the best. The ants are gone, crowds scattered; there is a refreshing novelty (and an art) to picnicking on a storm-smudged day. The weather is, in the forecaster's words, unsettled. If the day happens to be clear and bright, this is extra bounty: sharper views, black and white engraved landscapes.

Winter picnics can be had anywhere; they become events in the mountains and snow. Trees are white-bundled, the air has a chilly glint, people move inside a crystal paperweight. This is the time to eat thermos cups of hot chili, and sip minestrone, or drink mulled cider stirred with cinnamon sticks.

Skiing or tramping in the snow makes for vigorous appetites. Good for a tailgate picnic: impromptu fondue, reminiscent of Heidi and chalets and the entire Swiss mystique. The fondue is easy with one of the ready-prepared packaged varieties and large chunks of French bread. A not very Welsh rabbit is made of heated canned cheese soup lightly thinned with beer, with slabs of rye or pumpernickel for dunking.

In February, ranches and fields have a crisp austerity, a sharp grainy quality of black and white, like a photographic negative. Cows appear to stand brooding and motionless. A statement of authority to a country road, newly rediscovered; any outlook spot provides a subtly changed viewpoint to cloud-wrapped horizons. Familiar landmarks appear to have moved, looking, in the clear impersonal light of winter, farther away or astonishingly close at hand.

If the driving distance is not far, a hot casserole can be brought straight from the oven, well wrapped in aluminum foil—lasagne, or hot baked beans.

Winter picnics are for beaches.

Beaches now are totally deserted—except for stray hikers, birds, keening seagulls, a heron with lofty objectives. The waves are froth-bearded patriarchs leading to the shore.

Take cups of clam chowder from a seaside restuarant and eat in the car, security against the storm, or bring a thermos of Mexican oyster stew, spiced with olives and chili powder.

Some stretches of coastline—Washington and Oregon, for example—have a look of primeval simplicity, a kind of oriental sketchbook drawing with only an occasional thrust of cliff or a tangle of rocks showing in the insubstantial mist. Do wind and water carve out the rock niches, or do the cliff forms themselves alter and shape the storm? Dry red wine laced with tea is an accompaniment to sandwiches.

Winter picnics are for lakes. The day and the water are many shades of gray and the clouds are as full of foreboding as old biblical prophets. Parks are empty, picnic tables have an abandoned look.

Still, there are many moods in a short February day between the parentheses of frosty dawn and early twilight. Winter too is an adventure.

February 25

In some rural communities, particularly in New England, sleigh riding is still a pleasant custom. The practice conjures up a nostalgic scene: snow-covered roads and fields, tinkle of horses' bells, frosty breath on the air.

At night, there is a reversal of light values: the sky is dark and uninhabited; fields are alight with a faint glow. Bushes and trees merge in blackness, and shadows crowd everywhere.

Silence all around, in which sounds become meaningful: occasional hoarse hoot of an owl, or a random dog barking.

February in the world of nature is a time of indistinctness, of the blurring of familiar shapes, a look of remoteness now to unvisited roads and leafless trees. A season's spell of introspection and brooding; even the quietened earth has a look of meditation.

February 26

These are the early morning hours of the world. The first subtle stirrings of the land, as the pendulum returns. Most obvious sign:

the later, lingering twilight. Not much of a twilight—a short pallid interval—but the edges of the day are being pushed back. Fool's gold of a glittering dawn that (almost) promises a springlike day. Under the lengthening light, sluggish snowbound rivers move a little faster, as the sun melts a little of the snow. An occasional warm day, bright and clear as a windowpane, is a preview of what summer will be like. The snowdrop, precocious flower, makes its appearance. Someone calls a radio station: he has seen a pair of robins.

Small, inconspicuous signs are here and there that will be commonplace later but now seem significant and memorable; the first dandelion is also a splendid thing.

March 1

March can be considered only in charity a spring month; there is plenty of winter left, the bite and steel of cold wind, frost in the mornings, rain, a pallid wash-blue sky, sunshine with a nip in it. March is the meeting and duel of winter and spring. Spring starts forward, moves back; there are days of growth and non-growth. Yet the hours of light are lengthening.

March is for wearing boots and slickers and a wool scarf, and the next minute wondering if it isn't warm enough for a picnic after all. March is indecisive and captious, a fluttering change of mood with every racing cloud. Under sodden melting snow, new sprouts of green; tops of willow trees are brightening yellow. On a chilly day, the thin, sweet voice of the peeper, coolly piping from his place of concealment—a cautious Pan. Mad March hares in their riotous mating leap like spawning fish.

March 2

Patterns of March: Green buds, lean blades of grass, thrusting leaf shapes, thin-bladed snakes, clouds moving in schools, the leap and thrust of a kite.

March 3

All in their order: the bud, the leaf, the blossom, the fruit. In some trees, the flowers appear first: poplars, aspens, maples, oak, hickory, birch. More often, nature preserves the order, the old customary, proven sequence of growth, one reason evolutionary processes are so slow. Nature is the original concept of conservation; the new experiment or mutation is the accidental chance—the gamble against the odds.

March 4

Few mountain roads, despite the most calculated engineering, are entirely safe from the threat of avalanches. In nature, a strong pull exists to oust the intruder, to cover up the wound, to maintain the status quo. A new highway lies like a healing scar across the face of the mountains and minor snowslides block the road or spill rocks on treacherous corners; occasionally a major disaster occurs. To have walked such a road in the beginning of construction is to have seen a rape and destruction of the undisturbed: trees pulled up and out, great staring cuts of wood, a last glimpse of quiet wildness torn apart. Now in spring, the highway, or the railroad, is threatened.

The worst avalanche in railroad history occurred in 1910. Days of snowstorm had piled great drifts of snow in the Cascade passes, blocking traffic and burying roads; a passenger train and a mail train from Saint Paul were stopped near Stevens Pass in Washington. For almost a week passengers waited in the snowbound train. Snow turned to rain and an avalanche descended, ripping out trees and hurling rocks and snow down the slope. When the avalanche was over, the trains were destroyed and ninety-seven people were dead.

March 5

Wind is simply energy in motion, and in March the winds are bouncing, riding high, as tropical air races toward the poles and the cold polar air rushes to the equator. The buffeting of these purposeful opposites moves and leaps in almost play—March winds knóck hats off the dignified, turn umbrellas inside out, send papers flying down the streets. The great air masses race and lift; as the sun melts the pack of the northern snowfields the polar air loses its chilly power, but now the conflicts in these exaggerated temperatures of equatorial and polar air are at their extremes, and the brisk brawl ensues. March winds are conflicts and riots in the streets and in the fields.

Wind is moving atmosphere and can send temperatures dropping twenty degrees—the chill factor. The jostling colliding gales literally draw away heat. The brightest sunniest day in March means heat loss to the dance of the winds. Powerful, never still, the wind pulls and tugs at the earth and runs with it.

March 6

NAMES ON THE MOON

On a clear spring night, hundreds, thousands of stars bloom in the sky, white blossoms that make up a star garden. The clear moon looks uninhabited and remote, a pearl, a cool stone in the powdery flowering night.

The moon has been charted and named; to read the names is to speculate on unvisited and unimaginable places: the Abulfeda Crater, the Altai Escarpment, Brenner Crater-ring, Gutenberg Crater Basin (how the old printer would have loved that!), Gambert Hills, Harbinger Mountains, Heraclides Promontory, Mare Serenitas (Sea of Serenity) and those other strange seas, Mare Humorum (the Sea of Moisture), Mare Nectoris (Sea of Nectar), Mare Crisium (Sea of Crises). There is a Sea of Vapors, and a Straight Wall, a Mount Pico. Ancient Greeks and Romans share unconquered land: Archimedes Crater, Julius Caesar Crater, Aristoteles Crater. Impossible to think that the Spitzbergen Mountains are climbable; certainly no flowers bloom in the Alpine Valley. Who lives on the Carpathian Plateau?

To name a place is a human effort to give it permanency and a reality, even if it brings the place no closer or makes it no more habitable. It is as much a part of longing and ambition as to plant a flag on a desolate summit or a campsite in a desert.

Still, it is possible to conjecture, the moon has been there throughout the cooling years of an unguessed universe, and may have been visited by the others—those others who live in the far stations, the outposts of the night. The moon, possibly, belongs to them. And those craters and mountains invite a speculation: what are their *real* names?

March 7

CUPS OF GOLD

When the Spaniards first explored California they were amazed and delighted with the great flowing fields of tiny, golden cup-shaped flowers, the *copas de ora*. The California poppy—God's gold—flamed for miles along the coast and inland in the foothills. John Muir wrote: "When California was wild, it was the floweriest part of the continent. . . . So exuberant was the bloom of the main valley of the State . . . that in early spring, it was a smooth, evenly planted sheet of purple and gold, one mass of bloom more than four hundred miles long. . . ."

Now in March, the first poppies—the state flower—bloom along the highways and on curling hill slopes—a small, brilliant blossom, the color of the sun, and an open cup only to the sun, for it blooms only during the day.

The poppy family itself is large—over 115 varieties—but the California poppy grows only in California, except for a few random blooms in neighboring states.

Belatedly residents of the Golden State find that they have paved and placed oil wells and built the California poppy nearly out of existence; now a foundation exists to protect the poppy, and youngsters plant the poppies as part of school projects. The golden flower has become scarce, hard to find, and valuable.

March 8

THE TREES SPEAK

Clasp a young tree, and, standing close to it, listen attentively; there is at first silence, and then as the ears become sensitive and attuned, much as eyes grow accustomed to dimness, the sound of the tree itself. Heard most clearly in a young tree, it is a thin and reedy sound, a faint high-pitched humming, far away at first and then closer, not a wind sound, but the steady piped vibration of life and movement within the tree itself, the sound of rising sap and of cells breathing as the tree responds to air and light and water. Like the shell that traps air and thus seems to reproduce the sound of the sea, there is an audible breath in a young tree.

In silence, cling to a tree and listen to that sound. If winds move by and overhead, the tree seems a ship, anchored and at wait, and the voice is a command, Climb aboard!

March 9

The highest winds in the world blow on the summit of Mount Washington in New Hampshire.

People have started to hike up this New England mountain—an insignificant peak, a mere 6,288 feet, 150 miles from Boston, and have been buffeted and turned back by its cheerless atmosphere. Campers have died of avalanche injuries in Tuckerman Ravine, the arcing, crescent-shaped, glacier-carved open heart of the mountain. Hikers moderately well equipped for a spring or summer ramble have died of exposure on Washington's slopes.

There is hardly a best day, or a best time, for climbing Mount Washington; there are only days that are not as bad as others. More than half the time, the peak is covered with fog and drizzle. Every month of the year, snow falls. In the summer, the temperature manages to climb, haltingly, to a niggardly 73 degrees. Highest point of the northeast states, the rock-strewn summit is visited by winds of determination and ferocity; winds here have been clocked at 231 miles an hour.

Hardly a place to linger, the barren and unwelcoming summit, above the thin wind-bent trees and gray lichen and the polished granite.

True residents of Mount Washington: mosses and firs and spruce, beeches, rocks with the silent remote immensity of moon rocks, crashing, descending rivers and spilling streams, endlessly rushing down the sides of the mountain.

And in the spring, the slate-colored junco, nesting some-

times above timberline, high in the boulders, at home in swirling gray
mist and gray fog and gray stone.

March 10

Signs of spring appear first in the hardware and grocery
stores. Side by side with salt for driveways, and the Presto logs, appear
now new lawn mowers, bags of peat moss, bags of descented fertilizer.
Packets of flower and vegetable seeds make an appearance. Women in
boots, but with hair freshly curled, inspect the new offerings of garden
tools.

The day is raw and gray, and snow is still a real possibility in
most parts of the country, but *spring is on its way*. A million small retailers
can't be wrong. Particularly in rural areas, if a storm comes up tonight, it
means more days of semihibernation and waiting it out. March is a
chancy month for the existence of hope, but the proof of the season is
here. For millions of Americans, accustomed to a synthetic insulated
experience of sealed house and snug automobile, weather is something
that happens at a distance, to someone else, and the seasons are read in
the store displays.

March 11

The passion of nature is greening. Grass has an urgency;
dandelions spring up through the tiniest of crevices in driveways; this-
tles crack boulders like nuts. Weeds spill over the edges of lawns. A
compulsion and a competitiveness to all the green things soundlessly
jostling and fighting their way up to light and air. There may be in the
plant world, too, a territorial imperative; plants live (or fail to live, if they
do not win) in the space they claim as their own. The simplest process of
growth and life is the complex chain of events that begins with the
seizure of property. Cells need space in which to divide and multiply,
and on a March day, the bursting cells of plants claim and rearrange
space as if from the center of the earth, and drive upwards the property

stakes of green, in a blithe and exuberant resurgence. These are the owners of the earth.

March 12

The pussy willow comes into bloom now; along streams and fields the gentle catkins appear, soft as breath, the color of smoke. In this tree, the flower buds come first, heavily laden with pollen for early industrious bees.

In the parade of the year, this is the one peak moment for the otherwise inconspicuous shrub or small tree. For a few weeks, it is the very symbol, the plume of spring. A pussy willow to the touch is like soft fur—a bloom well clad for days of fog and mist.

March 13

THE GREAT SNAKE

Because the Shoshone Indians of the river plains identified themselves by placing the right hand at waist level, palm in, and moved the hand in a forward, paddling motion like swimming fish, the white men, missing the possible intent of the gesture (here the big fish runs) called the river the Snake. It has also been called the accursed mad river.

The Great Snake winds its rugged way down from Wyoming, west through southern Idaho, and then north, flowing along the Idaho, Oregon and Washington borders until it reaches the Columbia River.

Despite the dams built along the 1,038-mile course, the great river is still a splendid, wild, untamed thing. Twisting and swift-running, the sinuous waters swell from snowmelt in the Rockies in the spring, overflowing, leap down Shoshone Falls over the curving 1,000-foot basalt-rimmed drop. Along its route, the inhospitable white waters swirl; the river is born in wild country and is the home and route of wild things. Moose plunge across snow to cross the river; in the Snake River Canyon the golden eagle soars above the river and the steep squared walls of rock, free of trees. Weasels search for mice in the marshy riverbanks and grassy shoulders, and antelope roam in ancestral freedom in the fresh-smelling meadows. As it enters southern Idaho, the river is seized and trapped in a series of dams, furnishing energy for hydraulic power and irrigation for Idaho potatoes.

For 35 miles, the Snake is a dark and twisting thing; Hells Canyon is a gash in the land, a deep break savagely opened below the Seven Devils, old brooding rock mountains that sit at the edge of Idaho. For passing motorists who crawl the tortuous road, a dizzying look far down into a gorge deep and dark as death. Fifteen hundred feet deeper than the Grand, Hells Canyon carries the search of the mad river.

March 14

A grizzly bear is an impressive sight, a massive dish-faced, humpbacked beast who walks in his own great throne of fur; rising erect, a nightmare of small angry eyes in a vicious frame of power, long streaked claws, hatred and bad temper personified. No wonder he is called *Ursus horribilis*. To avoid the sight, hikers in Alaska carry tin cans of pebbles rattling at their waists and shiver respectfully if they see the immense prints of a grizzly's passing on the trail. In March, restless males are on the move, looking for mates. There are few grizzlies left (this is an animal not tolerated by man); a sparse number of survivors linger in Yellowstone and Glacier national parks.

The grizzly is a prototype, of course, of musty and primeval angers, a dim-brained and outraged patriarch, now dispossessed, and like all prototypes, doomed to extinction. Glimpsed across a river, or from several hundred yards of nervous safety, a grizzly is a better thing to look at: gleaming brown, expert fisher, a supple vision of strength.

With a perhaps undeserved reputation for ferocity—a grizzly has a shyness that will not tolerate the casual encounter—the great bear is ultimately the loser. In chance meetings with man and hand-to-hand encounters, the grizzly wins, but has paid ultimately with his life. In one of those uncanny coincidences which provoke the mind with their awful semblance of fate-charted destiny, and convince that the world is after all plotted and engineered by some captious god, two separate grizzlies, one hot night in Glacier National Park, mauled and destroyed two young girls many miles apart; one victim was partly eaten. Unthinkable, that the indifferent, garbage-eating beasts, staging nightly entertainment at the lonely mountain lodge, would ever turn on their friendly hosts. The National Park Service distinguished itself by advancing a number of theories, most of them preposterous, to account for this inconvenient tragedy. A girl ranger displayed a remarkably cold self-control, refusing to allow a search to proceed although the dying victim's moans could be heard in the darkness. Guests and campers were even worse; several retreated, rather than take part in the belated search, and others stood silently by when rescuers asked for jackets and clothing to warm the dying girl. A show of ingratitude, really, for all those evenings of entertainment at the garbage dump.

When the last of the bear carcasses had been hauled away, little more was known and nothing proved, except the now inarguable thesis that man and grizzly cannot coexist. No national park is a big enough refuge for the great bear.

The story of the grizzly in California is the bear's true biography and ultimately his epitaph. California seems a state largely populated by juvenile delinquents of all ages, intent on blackening the last stretches of coastline with oil refineries, and rendering extinct every living thing, including the condor and eventually man himself. At San Luis Obispo, grizzlies were at one time commonplace, viewed respectfully but with caution by the Indians; man and bear had coexisted in relative peace for thousands of years. With the white man's arrival, the grizzly lasted approximately three hundred years.

The Vizcaino expedition in 1602 were the first Europeans to see the grizzly, when they saw a bear feeding on a dead whale in a lonely bay. One hundred and seventy years later, the Portola expedition came upon a lone grizzly and promptly shot it.

For the next 150 years, the grizzly was shot, trapped, or used for entertainment; a bear would be pitted against a bull for some horrendous duel to titillate the enervated blood of prospectors and miners. Thus, the bull and bear of the stock market. In 1922, the last California grizzly was shot, and the pelt hung on a board at Horse Corral Meadows in Tulare County. The species—*Ursus arctos californicus*—has as habitat the state flag, and stands at the foot of the goddess Minerva on the great seal of the state of California.

Throughout the rest of the country, the grizzly will probably have an ever scarcer time of it as people increase and more roads are built threatening the grizzly's shrinking domain. After the Glacier Park incident, officials were known to lie awake at night, contemplating, Who are the national parks for, anyway?

A very few grizzly survivors—less than a dozen perhaps— have wandered down from Canada into the North Cascades National Park. Surly patriarch, dispossessed king, the grizzly lives on the thin edge of existence; man will not tolerate another beast who walks upright.

March 15

A restlessness to March; the changeable weather brings about a jittery impatience in winter-weary people. In past years, women engaged in frantic bouts of spring cleaning and are still known to make passes at moving furniture around. Men go out to play golf in bouts of streaming rain.

March 16

EDEN

The snakes appear. Sunshine is a bait, luring out the garter snake and the northern brown snake. The latter will spend much of his life lying under logs, or damp boards or stones, a creature timid of the light and fond of warmth.

The garter snake is a hardy, adaptable type, found around houses, barns, grassy hills, city parks—anywhere and everywhere.

People who feel called upon to defend snakes hold up the garter snake as beneficial, an eater of harmful insects. Actually the garter eats mainly toads, frogs, and earthworms.

Snakes have an unreliable look—glassy of eye and slithering about in a disconcerting, undependable manner. Their manner of locomotion and their unpredictable behavior give them a bad reputation. Like old roués, they startle young ladies, appearing suddenly in shrubs and dark corners; they look altogether too wiggly and unstable, with a disconcerting habit of creeping about, and display bad manners in their silence and tongue-flicking reticence.

As everyone knows who has held a snake, the body is surprisingly firm, with a dry papery feel; the snake is not slippery at all, except for a coiling determination to move out of harm's way.

The garter dislikes very much being surprised. Slender, pretty, a scaled jewellike green-brown, or smoothly striped, the snake can curl into an S of astonishment, or slide in a firm, winding getaway, all determination from the bright hard eyes to the flirt of tail. It grows to a respectable three feet, and has a liking for the fissures and crevices of the earth.

Hardy, fecund (20-50 young will be born of the March copulation near the den), the garter shows no sign of ever becoming a life-threatened species, but seems perfectly evolved and adapted to his stage of existence. Coolly and dryly the garters mate now, intent eye upon eye, meeting undisturbed and purposeful some thrusting command of instinct in the dim cycle of light and dark. The command is to replenish and multiply. A world without serpents would be unthinkable.

March 17

To fly a kite on a March day is a glad, light-hearted thing, totally frivolous and inconsequential, an art best practiced by little boys.

Just the right breeze is needed, a brisk, bouncy, spanking breeze that lightly disturbs the new leaves on trees and ruffles grass. The best kite may be a simple homemade one—a triangle of newspaper on a string-tied frame. It is possible to buy zippy plastic models, immense fluorescent wings, or sophisticated dragons (the orientals know what they are doing when they send up bright-colored flags to fend off the evil spirits).

On a mild day, an open field now becomes a parade of fluttering kites in all colors and symbols, the high-riding flags of childhood.

Launching is serious business. Only an amateur runs to get his kite airborne. Instead, the line is gracefully, flirtatiously unrolled—up to fifty feet—and the kite is offered to the breeze. Ideally, a vivacious breeze bends to take the kite up, but even if a series of faltering skips and dives are necessary, or even bringing the kite down to start over again, soon the kite will be gamboling toward the clouds.

The kite must be played out like a fishing line, in repeated small thrusts and skips. As the kite climbs it becomes steadier and purposeful in its flight, now at five hundred feet, now at six hundred. Once above the tricky little swells and pulls of ground breezes, the kite rides as grandly as a ship, controlled by gentle and earnest reeling in and out from the ground.

Flying a kite is serious, thoughtful work. A small boy cannot be asked to leave it too suddenly, to come in to dinner, for example; this breaks the train of thought and the flying kite must be connected always to the sober meditative mind on the ground, attentive to the tug of breeze, attuned to air currents, any change in the cloud pattern. A kite flyer has to be patient, and, above all, an optimistic pilot.

Kites sometimes get lost, or drift into trees, and end up as tangled, sorry things, helpless as marooned kittens. The best kite of all, the one that flies highest and farthest, is a memory, floating across a far field, reaching for the center of the sky, as personal as a dream.

Boys a little older improve on the game by kite-gliding, becoming air-borne themselves and gliding on the ends of kites down dunes at the beach, or steep slopes in the foothills. Large and impressively engineered kites are the requirement here, and careful footwork.

Businessmen, having done long ago with such nonsense, sit in offices and sail paper airplanes.

March 18

Spring fever was always a taken for granted occurrence, attributed variously to a scarcity of vitamins after a winter-sparse diet, or a lack of calcium, or a general human frailty. Grandmothers dosed youngsters with improbable concoctions—sulphur and molasses or quantities of rhubarb—and families urged each other to soak up the newly returned sunshine or wrap up warmly against March-changeable drafts. Young women drank tonics and forced their reluctant selves to go through the motions of work, stared moodily at the greening landscape.

In the face of nature's exuberance and fecundity, gamboling of lambs and chicks and swelling trees, such human languor seemed inexcusable, a thing to be set right with potions and will power.

Still, the delicious inertia persists, an almost-apathy, a weak and nodding vapory inattention; on a warm spring day there is a vast reluctance to move, or to accomplish anything much, a hesitancy and an unwillingness to be part of spring's action—reluctance in the face of revelation.

Spring fever has a metabolic basis. The lassitude is actually a temporary anemia. With warming temperatures and increasing light, the blood vessels dilate, and the blood is spread thin—a weak-pulsing blood that needs to adapt slowly to the heat and light of the season.

Best of spring tonics is an herb tea. Soothing and heartening is a tisane of valerian, or pennyroyal, sage, mint, camomile, rosemary, anise. A general rule for making herb teas: 1 teaspoon dried flowers or leaves to one cup of water, or 1 tablespoon fresh flowers or leaves. The tea is steeped five minutes, and served with lemon or honey. When soul and body feel weak and languid under the mounting pressure and excitement of spring, this is nourishment and revival.

March 19

Along streams, in damp meadows, on spring-nourished slopes, the Virginia bluebell comes into early blossom. Despite its name, this is a widely loved and welcomed spring flower from Ontario to Minnesota, from Nebraska to Kansas to South Carolina.

The pink buds blossom into bright blue and lavender bells, hanging in delicate clusters from the graceful stems. The life of the flower will be a short one; the seeds ripen and about a month after blossoming, the entire flower—oval leaves and fragile blossoms—dies. By the end of May, plus or minus a week or so, the delicate flower is gone.

March 20

GOD'S FAVORITE

At Yellowstone National Park, in a parking lot, a coyote slipped in and out of headlight beams, a wisp of fog-colored fur. Later the coyote sat atop jumbled rocks at the edge of trees and barked, yipped, howled, sang a little teeth-chattering scale. To people who heard him, he appeared to be laughing. "Crazy coyote!"

Quickly a coyote learns when he is—relatively—safe. Seizing the thin edge of advantage, he strolls in plain sight near office buildings at an Air Force base, or shows his teeth in that half-laugh. Yet a coyote absorbs quickly and well the fear of man into himself; nothing is more elusive than a coyote in the wild. He howls across a canyon or a lake in the dusk, a sliding plaintive howl-yip of sound, and is nowhere to be seen. To glimpse a coyote is to catch sight of a gray ghost.

God's dog, the Indians called him, and Hope Ryden gave that name to her study of the shy animal. As God's dog, the coyote is unwanted and despised by men, but endures. Even as an awkward gangly pup, all knock-knees and trembling nose, the coyote is learning resourcefulness and trigger-tense caution.

A full-grown coyote, slim-boned, narrow-faced, has a look of precocity like a clever child. His tawny fur appears grizzly and heavy for the slender legs; the eyes are intelligent and watchful; he can become invisible and at the same time see everything.

Like the wolf, the coyote is a social animal. Often a loner, hunting and working alone, he will nevertheless form companionships with other coyotes, and deep and fruitful bonds with a mate: litters average half a dozen but may run as high as twelve or even fourteen. Friendly neighbors in the pack often help raise the pups and help teach the behavior of stealth and caution. Albino coyotes are scarce, occurring most often in the Far West states, perhaps, an evolutionary mistake with no survival value.

The pup catching mice and insects soon becomes a resourceful and purposeful adult. He crawls on his belly to sniff at dead animals; traps or poison may be concealed in that attractive bait. Few coyotes work harder than they have to: carrion, jackrabbits, ailing deer and elk are easy meals. Coyotes do not waste their energies attempting to bring down healthy, full-grown, large animals. Occasionally domestic lambs or chickens are taken—easy pickings for the clever and agile coyote. He is an opportunist who doesn't miss a chance.

Men have made an earnest attempt to rid the world of God's

dog. In the fight against the coyote, people, mostly ranchers and sheepmen, have put as much money and effort as a medium-sized war. In 1966, government trappers "controlled" 78,000 coyotes and the figures continue to rise. The U.S. Forest Service, under the Department of Agriculture, has been particularly vulnerable to the enraged cries of stockmen that they are losing their flocks to the canny coyote, and money quietly changes hands, and millions of dollars are spent in the determination to exterminate the coyote.

The methods used are not gentlemanly. Poison is a favorite tool: cyanide, strychnine, and the ignominious 1080 have killed millions of coyotes on public lands—in the process killing also eagles, foxes, bobcats, endangered species, ranch dogs, and now and then a human. The use of non-selective poisons has been (temporarily) halted; powerful lobbying interests fight to resume poisoning, and individuals often continue it illegally. For God's dog, devilish treatment: ingenious, if heavy-handed ranchers have strung up living coyotes and pulled the bladders out of the suffering animals to use as bait to lure other coyotes. A farmer in Kansas boasted that he had killed "every coyote for miles around and then some." His bumper sticker reads: "Support the American farmer. Kill a coyote today." Residents of South Dakota have totally succeeded in killing the coyote, their state animal; it is extinct there. Between 1972 and 1973, federal control agents trapped, shot from

airplanes and helicopters, and otherwise destroyed 10,000 more coyotes than they had poisoned in the previous year.

The coyote is the underdog, living by his running-scared wits, shadowy pursuer of the sick deer, the starving antelope. As a scavenger, he is an agent of natural and efficient selection. He clears the lands of rats, gophers, and other harmful rodents, and gets for thanks a bullet or a lingering death torn bloodily between the jaws of a trap.

In a few areas, the number of coyotes has declined, but elsewhere the coyote persists; Indians believed that the coyote will be the last animal on earth.

At dusk, his voice lifts in a half-mournful, half-taunting solo and is joined by other calling, trembling voices, coming from all directions at once, now near, now distant. His tracks are doglike in the snow—a thin shadow scurries, tail down, across a field; elusive ghost-eyes glow in the woods darkness. Given a quarter of a chance, the coyote may yet survive, out of sheer wits and willpower, and, maybe, a helping chance from the thing whose dog he is.

The coyote may yet have the last laugh.

March 21

The first day of spring is the event the early astronomers called the vernal equinox. Now the sun enters and crosses the sky's equator, an imaginary line drawn through the heavens directly above the equator of the earth. The sun moves now toward the furthest northern point of its travels, and spring comes to the northern hemisphere. Days lengthen, the earth warms, the runner has led the way.

Officially, spring has arrived. But as often as not the first day of spring is chilly and veiled, a cloudy anticlimax to more promising days. In nature, lines are blurred; there are no black and white calendar days. But under the beating rains, the clock ticks the slow and measured advance of spring as the sun goes north, bringing birds in its wake; happenings are fast. Spring is the swiftest time, when growth is most visible and changes most frequent. This is the season—not the day—when everything happens at once.

March 22

"These things give me comfort," the old Indian said, "the coyote, the eagle . . ."

"An affinity for doomed things, perhaps?"

The old Indian shook his head slowly. He had the crumbly brown look that some Indians possess who have lived long in the sun. Under hard empty New Mexico dawns only their eyes seem alive, bright and blue, and the sun beats down like a spotlight.

"Things are not doomed. They change and go away and reappear. They always come back." He held up a basket, into which was woven the face of the sun.

March 26

Frogs lay their eggs. Soon tadpoles will dart and scurry in ponds that are the bustling laboratories of life.

March is a number of small things: a jeweler's case of tiny insects, beetles emerging, small and black as punctuation marks; trillium, tiny buds emerging; precocious crocus; the fairy shrimp, swimming in a pool, his beating tiny heart clearly visible; whitlow grass, with flowers so small that they are invisible to the casual passerby.

The energy in small things is tremendous; an immense exuberance of life spills and burgeons in the little creatures—all the small, frail things that prove survival is in numbers.

The weak will inherit the earth.

March 27

A black bear emerges from her den, sleepy and cross, leading two tiny bear cubs and blinking in the shadowed woods light.

After the long sleep, a mother bear is in no mood to be trifled with, not with her cubs nearby, as several hikers and campers have sadly learned.

Part of a bear's appeal is its look of droll, stumbling gaucherie. But the woods clown can move fast, and maternal instinct—a temporary, hormone-triggered reflex of nerves and muscles—is a powerful incentive.

The cubs are born in winter, scarcely disturbing the mother's long sleep. At birth, the black bear is a hairless, helpless creature weighing less than half a pound, a tiny scrap of living flesh, small enough to ride in a man's hand. He will grow to weigh 200 to 500 pounds.

Emerging in the spring, the cub follows dutifully at his mother's side, eager and confused with new smells and sounds and a spicy forest world to gambol in. Charming and feckless, little black bears gave Theodore Roosevelt pause: "I'll hold my fire for anything that cute." The Teddy bear became a plaything, subject of a book, a memory, an entire era of nostalgia.

Good climbers, the cubs can take to trees at their mother's command. Her stinging paw enforces discipline if they are slow to obey, or explore too far. Childhood will be short; a bear quickly learns the close dimensions of his world. Adult bears may scarcely roam more than a couple of miles from the homesite—and the shadow shapes and forms of his limited world: the dim trees, the stream, the berries and the fish, the narrow way of survival.

March 28

The migrant birds return.

A welcome for: robins, mourning doves, redwings, bluebirds, blackbirds. Familiar voices fill the air. Homecoming! But these early arrivals coming home mean departures, too. The others are leaving, slipping away so silently and unnoticed that only after awhile is their absence noticed. Spring is loss as well as gain. They are leaving: the tree sparrow, the chickadee, the nuthatch. The snow bunting has gone north.

March 30

It is a green hollow where a stream sings
    Crazily hooking itself on grasses into silver shreds.

And where from his proud mountains shines the Sun
Down into a tiny valley bubbling with luminescences.
–Arthur Rimbaud

March 31

Trees are the original prophets.
In March, the swelling bud foretells the season. Woodsmen read bark and moss for signs, and some old-timers look for early-turning leaves to warn them of a hard winter. In very old trees—the great sequoias, the sky-nudging redwoods—careful observers see a wisdom of the earth made manifest, visible memories of ice ages and giants. Trees are the original wise men, and their gifts are shelter to animals and birds, and strength and support to the soil. In the shade of a tree, Indian braves drew a sense of strength and courage; the young Indian boy, fasting, climbed to a tree nest to await the dream-vision that told what his role in life would be. A little boy dreaming on a tree limb gets a feeling of what it will be like to be as tall as a man.
Hoarse-voiced in a high spring wind, swaying and grunting, trees are old soldiers defending the line.

And the seed is awakening, beginning to grow;
for the year neither ends nor begins
but simply changes,
and time (the stuff of life) is granted
to those who travel for a while
the shoulder of the moving and patient wheel
which turns forever.